YOUR MOST
POWERFUL
WEAPON

How to Use Your Mind to Stay Safe

Steve Tarani

TARANI

"There is a middle ground between denial and Jason Bourne. Steve has provided a road map to get there. "

COLONEL STEVEN P. BUCCI, PH.D.
Former United States Undersecretary of Defense

ACKNOWLEDGEMENTS

In sincere gratitude for your most generous contributions to this four-year work effort. Listed in alphabetical order:

Denise M. Bixler

Dr. Steven P. Bucci

Christopher DiCenso

Doug Esposito

Gary Greco

Paul Grybow

Patrick Henry

Guro Dan Inosanto

Mike McBee

Penny Maurer

Thomas Petrowski

Tom Rovetuso

Kelly Schwartz

Barry Shreiar

Michael Vaiani

Bill Werntz

TABLE OF CONTENTS

HOW TO USE YOUR MIND TO STAY SAFE

In a world where terrorist attacks, active shootings, and physical violence are the new normal, how can you keep you and your family safe *without* a firearm or knowing martial arts?

What if you already carried an effective weapon with you, every day, and only needed to learn how to use it?

Your most powerful weapon – your mind – is at your disposal 24/7. It doesn't need a permit or batteries, and never runs out of bullets. Carried with you everywhere, it can be deployed quick as thought – *if you know how*.

Your Most Powerful Weapon teaches you how to: build mental toughness, control your environment, avoid a threat, defeat an attack, and control fear.

What people say about *Your Most Powerful Weapon*:

"I didn't realize how little I had to learn to be so much safer."

"It changed my personal outlook which changed my reality."

"I thought I was going to be intimidated, but now I feel intimidating!"

AUTHOR'S BIO

Steve Tarani is a former CIA full-time employee, protective services subject matter expert who served on Donald Trump's pre-election executive protection detail, and is the lead instructor for a nationally-recognized awareness-based training program offered to nearly 3 million members. Tarani, an active protective agent, is a Central Intelligence Agency and FLETC certified federal instructor who also provides services for the US Naval Special Operations Command, FBI National Citizens Academy Alumni Association, National Association of School Resource Officers (NASRO), and others.

FACING THE NEW NORMAL

Today we face a "new normal". This is radically different from what I grew up with, or even the world I "patrolled" as a life-long Army Green Beret. Every day, we face the threat of terrorism: as we travel around the world or whenever we visit a large prominent city, AND even in small town America. The threat has never been greater, or more likely to pop up anywhere.

As I travel the United States speaking on security issues of all sorts, I am constantly asked two things; "Is the threat real?" and "What can I do?" The answer to the first is an emphatic "Yes." The foundational answer to the second is "Use your mind". Steve Tarani's superb book is the extended version of that second answer.

Before I say anything else, I want to immediately answer all those who would challenge that this sort of book and this sort of mind set are calls for fear and individual isolation.

My reply is a simple one – preparation does not provoke paranoia; it prevents it.

As mentioned, I spent a long Army career as a Special Forces Colonel. I served in Eastern Europe, the Balkans, Latin America, Africa and the Middle East leading some of the best warriors America has in very difficult and dangerous places and situations. Danger and preparedness for it are not strange to me. Despite that, on September 11th, 2001 I was as surprised as everyone else. I was in the Pentagon that day, serving as the Military Assistant to the Secretary of Defense, Donald H. Rumsfeld.

Like the rest of America and the world, we saw the plane hit the first World Trade Center tower, and thought "Oh my, what a tragedy!" Then we saw the "replay"; except it was not a replay, but the second plane. In the epicenter of America's defense establishment, we looked at each other in silence for a moment, and knew this was a deliberate act; we were at war. We sprang into action, but literally a few short minutes later, our building was hit as well. The fight with terrorism had truly come home to America.

As a military professional whose specific field includes countering terrorism, I knew this war had started long before that fateful day (first World Trade Center bombing, the U.S.S. Cole bombing, and Al Qaeda's open declaration of war of the U.S.), but 9/11 made it real for all of America. Subsequent acts of terrorism (Major Nidal Hassan's attack at Ft. Hood, TX, the attempted Times Square bombing, shootings in Orlando, FL and San Bernardino, CA, and the Boston Marathon bombing, just to name a few) further hammered this home. Al Qaeda's continued threats against us, joined now with ISIS and all their affiliates are clear and unambiguous. They will never stop, negotiate, or concede. They are in a fight to the finish, and like it or not so are we.

This book is not really about the big picture political and military challenges facing America, but such challenges have created the context in which Steve Tarani is now working. His concepts are designed to help us all operate safely and as normally as we can in this context.

America has been blessed with such security and peace at home, for so long that we assume tranquility is, and should be, the norm. That is no longer the case. Unfortunately, even facing a threat that can and does strike in seemingly random places, at completely unconnected times; we as citizens drift into La La Land far too frequently. As I execute security assessments and teach security classes nationwide, in churches, schools, small businesses, and communities, I always get the question, "Surely this could never happen here?" Sadly, the answer is "Yes, it can, and it is growing more likely every day."

One has only to think about any of the examples noted earlier to see the validity of my response. I would challenge the reader to think of the airport security officer in Flint, MI, a small, local airport, standing outside the security "ring". A Canadian citizen, who had earlier driven into the U.S. through New York State, entered the airport, pulled a large knife, screamed "Allahu Akbar", and stabbed the officer in the neck. No one thought it would happen there.

It can happen anywhere, at any time.

So how can you be prepared for this? Steve Tarani is a big, imposing, and highly skilled warrior. He is a nationally recognized expert in every sort of defensive methodology. He can use rifles, pistols, knives, and improvised weapons, even his hands, all with deadly proficiency. That said, Steve's greatest asset is without a doubt, his mind. His most effective "technique" is his ability to think his way out of bad situations, or even better, to *proactively* avoid the problem in the first place. And, he does it without walking around in a perpetual state of blind fear or an adrenalin fueled, never blinking, paranoia. He lives his life, loves his family, and serves his fellow citizens with a kind and gentle demeanor that completely belies his capabilities. He wants to share that with all of us.

What Steve has compiled in "Your Most Powerful Weapon", is a gold mine. It is readable, understandable, and applicable for all of us, the regular folks. Frankly, that is not the norm for so many books on personal security. Most require you to become Steve Tarani to be of any use. That is a tough bar folks (actually, it is impossible), but learning and using what Steve himself has compiled is within our grasp. That is why he is considered a master instructor.

This volume will break down the present-day situation (potentially grave threats coming when we least expect them), teach you how to prepare for it (control your environment, control the threat, defeat the attack), and above all else survive (control your fear). Not everyone will be able to be stronger and faster than every threat. You may not want to carry a weapon (or be able to do so legally), or to achieve master levels of proficiency. You also do not want to lock yourself and your family away to be safe.

I suppose you could just ignore it all, like a small child, who thinks if they just cover their eyes, the scary thing goes away. I do not recommend that. That is La La Land. There is a middle ground between denial and Jason Bourne. Steve has provided a road map to get there. This goal is a worthy one, regardless if one is thinking high-level policy, or individual personal security. In my experience, at both levels, this type of thinking is sorely needed.

Again, I must repeat, in caps this time: PREPARATION DOES NOT PROVOKE PARANOIA, IT PREVENTS IT! If you apply Steve's concepts to engage that most powerful weapon we carry with us always; the mind, you can get there. You can move through life better protected and still be at peace. Should that not be our goal? It is mine, and the one I have tried to pass on to my sons as they raise, lead, and protect their own families. I sincerely hope it is yours as well.

This book will get you there. Enjoy it. Learn from it. Live it.

Colonel Steven P. Bucci, Ph.D.
Former United States Undersecretary of Defense
U.S. Army Special Forces (ret.)
De Oppresso Libre (To Free the Oppressed)

INTRODUCTION

Given the increased intensity and frequency of terrorist attacks, active shootings, bombings and other bad things that happen to good people these days, it makes you wonder; what would you do if it happened to you?

As a personal security instructor, I'm often asked "What can I do to protect myself and my family from these things?" The answer is, there's lots you can do, and you don't need any prior experience, a karate chop, big muscles or a firearm to be tremendously effective.

People who ask that same question, also expect a one-word answer and I wish there was one. However, the problem with which we are challenged, is not an easy one. The more you know, the more you understand why you cannot expect a simple answer to such a complex problem. If there were a one-word answer, then we would all know it and physical violence would cease to exist!

Ignorance

People fear what they don't understand. Your greatest challenge is not the threat itself, but ignorance of what it is, and how to deal with it. The most effective approach to this problem is education – there's no shortcut around it. Knowing exactly what you're up against, how to exploit your attackers' weaknesses, and how to use that knowledge to your advantage, is what it takes to meet the challenge. Armed with your most powerful weapon – your mind – you can learn how to defend against undesired events that may impact your own personal security and that of your family.

As a federal contractor, I am hired to train unarmed personnel who are preparing to go on assignment in very nasty places. The training is a pre-deployment package consisting of non-physical personal security skills. These people have no access to firearms, or other weapons. Should they find themselves in harm's way, both on and off duty, they must rely solely on these skills using nothing but their most powerful weapon,

If you are active/ former military or a sworn officer, odds are you may be familiar with some of this information. However, some of it may be new and you may very well appreciate the layered approach, organization, and integrated content, designed to support and assist your efforts in disseminating this valuable information to your inner circle.

Peek Behind the Curtain

If you have no federal agency, military or law enforcement background, then this is designed *specifically* for you! You get a sneak peek behind the tier-one protective services curtain, and an opportunity to benefit from the same "gray man"[1] training provided to active members of the U.S. defense intelligence community.

---

1   "Gray Man" is a term attributed to the Defense Intelligence community describing persons trained in the art of blending into the environment as part of the performance of their job.

Protection professionals will tell you that your mind is your most effective weapon. Knowing what to look for, how to look for it, and what to do if you see it, is paramount to anything else. In most situations, you can remain proactive and take preventative measures against a potential threat.

You're in the Right Camp

Our society is divided into two groups: those who don't care about, or are unaware of, the increasing likelihood that something bad can happen to them, and are unprepared to handle it, versus those who are aware and prepared if something bad happens. Learning how to use your most powerful weapon places you in the latter group, and prepares you by increasing your knowledge and decreasing your vulnerability.

CHAPTER 1

SITUATION NORMAL

"Today we face a new normal."

COLONEL STEVEN P. BUCCI, PH.D.
Former United States
Undersecretary Of Defense

The New Normal

The United States Department of Homeland Security calls anything bad that can happen to you anywhere or anytime an "*Active Threat.*" What exactly does this mean? An *active threat* can be anything from an act of terrorism such as an active shooter at work, at school, when you're out shopping or at a movie theater, at a music concert, detonation of an explosive device, a knife attack, a truck driving through a crowd of people or some such similar violence. It can include crimes such as a mugging, kidnapping, rape, home invasion, cyber-attacks, identity theft and random acts of physical violence.

Active threats occur so frequently now that only the headliners make the news. We, as a society, become more desensitized to them as they become more commonplace. Regardless of how desensitized we may be, violent physical attacks on people who are unaware and unprepared for them, are considered the new normal. Those who are unaware and unprepared for an *active threat* are viewed as *soft targets*[2] by those planning to do the killing.

Recent history demonstrates there has been a significant increase in such attacks on *soft targets* globally.[3] What lessons can you learn from these attacks to better prepare yourself and your family for the next one?

In the United States Defense Intelligence community, physical assaults resulting in death or severe bodily injury are divided into two general categories – those attacks conducted *with leadership* and those conducted *without leadership*.

Attacks conducted *with leadership* are, for the most part, highly organized, have many participants (called "actors") and usually involve long periods of preparation time.

---

2   Potential victims, easy marks for the terrorist, criminal or opportunist.
3   http://dennismichaellynch.com/fbi-investigations-radical-terrorists-alarming/

Such attacks involve specialized equipment to include higher technology weapons such as bombs (improvised explosive devices or IEDs) and/ or semi or fully automatic firearms. They also involve multiple actors coordinating pre-attack activities using cell phones, on-line communications, making physical observations and determinations about their target location (conducting pre-operational surveillance) and running dry-run walk throughs (red cell probes) to test targeted site security measures.

The bad news is that if these attacks are successful, they can be devastating and impact hundreds or even thousands of innocents. The good news is that federal agencies and local law enforcement have dedicated counter-terrorism resources, to include counter-surveillance and *Protective Intelligence*[4] units, to go after these actors and stop the threat before it happens.

Outside the purview of the average citizen, detecting and disrupting attacks *with leadership*, although usually met with a high rate of success, is an arduous and full-time occupation for the professionals. We don't often see these successes in the news as to protect their methods and practices.

At the exact opposite end of the spectrum are attacks conducted *without leadership* also known as "lone wolf" attacks. Although perhaps inspired by a monitored organization – what counterterrorism experts call "enabling" or "controlling", the lone wolf predominantly operates per his namesake without any direct supervision.

---

4   https://www.ncjrs.gov/pdffiles1/nij/179981.pdf

Usually with no other actors and often with minimal or no funding, the lone wolf is forced to do everything himself. He must select a location, prepare for the attack, acquire the necessary equipment and support materials. Given lack of direct guidance, funding and experience, the tools of the trade of a lone wolf are usually low tech such as a knife[5] or axe[6] or even a truck.[7]

Given the lone wolf's lack of training and experience, he is considered an amateur by the experts and as such is prone to making amateur mistakes such as inadvertently exposing his nefarious activities.

The bad news is that if lone wolf attacks are successful, they can impact a significant number of bystanders. The good news is, although too small a fish that usually slips through the nets of dedicated state agency counter-terrorism efforts, the lone wolf is prone to the watchful eyes of the prepared, aware and observant – also known as *hard targets.*

Terrorists, predators, active shooters, etc., (aka bad guys), especially lone wolves, go after lower hanging fruit. They purposely seek out *soft targets* and steer clear of *hard targets* – which have a very high likelihood of burning or hurting them, or otherwise disrupting their plans. Go

---

5   On August 3, 2016, the 64-year-old wife of an American professor was killed and five others injured in a knife attack in central London's Russell Square in what police called a "spontaneous" assault.

6   On July 19, 2016, a teenage Afghan refugee armed with an *axe* and knife injured four people on a train in Wurzburg Germany before being shot dead by police.

7   On July 14, 2016, 85 people were killed and 307 injured when a 19-ton cargo truck was deliberately driven into crowds celebrating Bastille Day in Nice, France.

online and you can find many cases of hard targets foiling attempted terrorism[8], home invasion[9] or child abduction[10] by the lone wolf.

Yes, we do live in a dangerous world, and it is part of our reality today, that we must think about what we would do if we were caught in an active threat. However, most people don't know, don't want to know, or don't care. They think "It will never happen to me or my family." If it ever does, then they think "Someone else will handle it." They cannot wrap their mind around the fact that their own personal security is *their* responsibility and that the new normal is a fact of life today. Why is that?

Normalcy Bias

Your most powerful weapon serves many functions for you other than that of a weapon. One of these functions includes making you feel safe and protected. Others include deciding what to wear, remembering where you put your keys, scheduling appointments and the like. However, if needed to be used as a weapon, it must first be made ready for deployment by switching modes from these routine tasks.

Much like a handgun which is retained in a holster, your mind is retained by a non-physical retention mechanism. To use your mind as a weapon, it must first be disengaged

---

8   http://www.csmonitor.com/USA/Military/2011/0729/Accused-Fort-Hood-plotter-got-bombmaking-recipe-from-Al-Qaeda

9   http://wtov9.com/news/local/quick-thinking-helps-wintersville-woman-foil-break-in

10   http://www.fox25boston.com/news/brockton-boys-quick-thinking-stops-possible-abduction/209860161

from this mechanism. To do that, you need to know what it is, how it works and then how to defeat it when necessary. This retention mechanism is called *Normalcy Bias*.

What is *Normalcy Bias*? Initially hypothesized by Charles E. Fritz in 1961 as "social and personal factors…which influence interpretations of danger messages and cues," *Normalcy Bias* is a mental state you enter when confronted with an overwhelming threat. It makes you disbelieve your situation when faced with grave and imminent danger.[11] This phenomenon causes you to greatly underestimate the severity and the most likely consequences. This, in turn, causes you to *reinterpret* the event, instead of taking evasive or decisive action.

An historical example of *Normalcy Bias* dates as far back as the ancient Roman resort city of Pompeii where in August 29AD Mount Vesuvius literally blew its top, spewing tons of molten ash, volcanic rock and sulfuric gas miles into the atmosphere. A firestorm of poisonous vapors and molten debris engulfed the surrounding area, suffocating the inhabitants of the neighboring cities of Herculaneum and Stabiae until nothing remained to be seen of the once-thriving communities.

Who was the brain trust that decided to build less than six miles from the base of an active volcano when there were warnings for seventeen years prior in the form of earthquakes and toxic gases being released through fissures in the rock powerful enough to kill livestock?

---

11   International Journal of Mass Emergencies and Disaster, Nov. 1988, Vol 6, No. 3, PP 315

History tells us that natural hot springs are what attracted the first inhabitants.

Near to the eruption date in August 79AD, Vesuvius started coming to life. Pliny the Younger[12] whose letters described his experience during the eruption while he was staying at the nearby home of his Uncle Pliny the Elder[13] recorded the events of this increased activity. He wrote that the Romans were not particularly alarmed because the earthquakes were so frequent. *Normalcy Bias* assured them they had nothing to worry about and that everything was going to be just fine.

Per Pliny the Younger, the residents of Pompeii had become accustomed to the quakes. Four days prior to the eruption, the earthquakes began to increase in frequency. Noxious air, falling volcanic rock and multiple quakes continued to harass townsfolk but these "normal" warnings were not heeded.[14]

On Aug 24th 79 AD the first eruption was a high-altitude ash column. At this point, some of the population interpreted this as a definitive warning and fled. The majority, influenced by *Normalcy Bias*, did not.

It was the next day, August 25 79AD, when the main eruption began. Pyroclastic flow of 600 degrees moved at 450 mph toward the base. Those remaining near the volcano were killed in a split second. At this point, there

---

12   Gaius Plinius Caecilius Secundus, born Gaius Caecilius or Gaius Caecilius Cilo (61 – c. 113), was an Ancient Roman lawyer, well-known author, and magistrate.

13   An official in the ancient Roman court in charge of the fleet stationed at the Bay of Naples and a naturalist.

14   *Pliny the Younger, Letters 6.16 and 6.20 to Cornelius Tacitus*

was no longer opportunity to escape. An estimated 16,000 people remaining in the city were killed. The cities remained buried and undiscovered for almost 1,700 years until excavation began in 1748.

One of the most tragic examples of the devastating effects of *Normalcy Bias* occurred less than two hundred years after that excavation. Where, at the onset of Nazi Germany, despite increasing persecution, including official discrimination, harassment, and oppression, many Jews decided to stay.

August 2005, despite sufficient warning from authorities, many residents of the city of New Orleans, Louisiana, failed to evacuate the area where hurricane Katrina hit, causing the deaths of 1,245 people and $108 Billion in property damage.

As humans, we don't want to feel anxiety or fear. We cling to what is familiar and comfortable. *Normalcy Bias* is a self-soothing, subconscious response to danger as to lower our anxiety and fear. In this mental state, we reinterpret new information and new situations so they become, in some way, normal and non-threatening to us.

The first statistical example of *Normalcy Bias* occurred on October 23, 2002 during the Nord-Ost Siege in the Dubrovka area of Moscow about four kilometers south-east of the Moscow Kremlin. During Act II of a sold-out performance, a little after 9:00PM, 40-50 heavily armed Chechen terrorists drove a bus to the theater and entered the main entrance hall firing rifles into the air. The black and camouflage clad Chechens took approximately 850-900 hostages, including members of the audience and performers.

Reaction of the spectators inside the theater to the news that the theater was under terrorist attack was not uniform. The response of the hostages ranged from calm to hysterical and some even fainted. Although the terrorist entered the theater in black balaclavas, camouflage and with guns blazing, most of the audience though it was part of the show. This thinking is not a rational or conscious decision, but *Normalcy Bias* providing assurances that everything is OK.

In all, some 90 people, about 10% of the hostages, managed to flee the building or hide. The remainder entered a catatonic state, came unglued, or fainted. Most people think "Well, I'd never do that! If I was faced with that situation I would simply spring in to action and do what it would take to solve the problem!" You certainly *hope* that this would be the case, but research suggests otherwise.

British psychologist John Leach at the University of Lancaster, states in a 2004 article published in Aviation, Space, and Environmental Medicine[15] "People who find themselves caught up in a natural disaster [Pompeii, Katrina] or violent physical threat [Nazi Germany, Dubrovka, Russia] tend to fall into three categories."

When disaster strikes, Leach says, we transform from our normal selves to our crisis selves. In one category, about 10-15% remain calm and act quickly and efficiently. In his book *Survival Psychology*,[16] he states; "These people will be able to collect their thoughts quickly, their awareness of the situation will be intact, and their judgement and

---

15   Today published as Aerospace Medicine and Human Performance.
16   *Survival Psychology*, John Leach, Pagrave MacMillan (UK), 1994

reasoning abilities will not be impaired to any signifi-cant extent."

In another category, 85-90% become "stunned, bewil-dered and uncertain of what to do next" (Leach), at the effect of *Normalcy Bias*.

The remaining category, 10-15% will go into blind panic ["uncontrolled weeping, confusion, screaming and par-alyzing anxiety" (Leach)], finding it impossible to reason during a catastrophic event and further attenuating the likelihood of their survival.

CATEGORY	PERCENTAGE	CONDITION
1	10-15%	Calm and Effective
2	85-90%	Influenced by *Normalcy Bias*
3	10-15%	Blind Panic

Fig. 1. Response Categories

What determines which category you fall into? You might expect decisive people to be assertive and flaky people to unravel. But when nothing is normal, the rules of everyday life do not apply, and *Normalcy Bias* prevails.

It's important to note the difference between "flight, fight or freeze" options influenced by *fear*, covered in later chapters, and *Normalcy Bias* – where you become ab-normally calm, and your mind reinterprets your situation assuring you that everything is normal when disaster hits. These are two very different phenomenon affecting human behavior in disasters.

No one knows more about human behavior in disasters than researchers in the aviation industry. Because they must comply with so many regulations, they run thousands of people through experiments and interview scores of crash survivors. Of course, a burning plane is not the same as a flaming skyscraper, a terrorist attack in a nightclub or active shooter at an outdoor country music concert. But some behaviors in all three environments turn out to be remarkably similar.

On March 27, 1977, a Pan Am B-747, was taking off at Los Rodeos Airport at Tenerife, Canary Islands off the coast of Spain. It was ripped open without warning by another B-747, a Dutch KLM jet, which came hurtling out of the dense fog at 160 miles per hour. Altogether, 583 of the 644 passengers and crew aboard the two planes died.[17] Everyone on the KLM jet was killed when the plane crashed down. However, it appeared as if many of the Pan Am passengers had survived and would have lived if they had gotten up and walked off the fiery plane.

Captain Robert Bragg (1937 – 2017) was the co-pilot aboard the *Pan Am* plane, and was one of the few who survived the incident. In an after-action report he stated, "I thought he'd [pilot of the KLM jet] just glanced over us because it was a very slight shake, very slight sound 'thump' and that was about it." His mind had assured him that it was only a bump. Reverting to his training, he reached up for the power control handles located above the pilot's head to shut down and cut the fuel to the engines.

---

17   "Spaniards Analyze Tenerife Accident," *Aviation Week* and *Space Technology*, Nov. 20, 1978, pages 113-121

"That's when I noticed that the top of the airplane was gone." In the same report he recalls, "I could see all the way to the tail of the airplane. It was like someone had taken a big knife and just sliced the top of the airplane off."[18] Realizing the true gravity of the situation he was able to take further action to save lives.

Dr. Daniel Johnson, a human factor psychologist, interviewed several survivors of the incident. Two of them were Paul and Floy Heck. Floy Heck, then 70, was sitting on the Pan Am jet between her husband Paul and her friends. After the KLM jet sheared off the top of their plane, Floy could not speak or move. "My mind was almost blank. I didn't even hear what was going on," she told an Orange County Register reporter years later. After a moment, her husband Paul got up and started toward the exit. As he left his seat he told his wife, "Follow Me!" At first Mrs. Heck sat in her seat doing nothing. She later remembered, "This is it." She thought she was going to die but she was not afraid. She says she was in a daze, but after her husband yelled, "Follow me!" She got out of her seat and moved into the isle. She followed him through the smoke "like a zombie", she said.

The Hecks were travelling with another couple, the Larsons, who were seated directly across the aisle from them. Just before they jumped out of a hole in the left side of the aircraft, Floy looked back at her friend Lorraine Larson, who was just sitting there, looking straight ahead, her mouth slightly open, hands folded in her lap. Like the many other passengers Floy observed just sitting there,

18   http://www.project-tenerife.com/engels/PDF/robertbragg.pdf

Lorraine would die not from the collision but from the fire that came afterward. Apparently, many of the people, at least in this section of the aircraft were behaviorally inactive.[19]

Dr. Johnson explained. "The [Hecks] said that many more people could have survived this accident had they simply moved from their seats and gone to the exists. [Floy] felt that she would have died had it not been for her husband telling her to follow. They both agreed that a major reason for their survival was the attention they paid to the flight attendant's briefing."[20]

We tend to assume that plane crashes, terrorist attacks or other acts of extreme physical violence are binary; you live or you die, and you have very little choice in the matter. However, in all serious U.S. plane accidents from 1983 to 2000, just over half of the passengers lived, per the National Transportation Safety Board. And some survived because of their individual traits or behavior — human factors, as crash investigators put it. After the Tenerife catastrophe, aviation experts focused on those human factors, like the Hecks, and decided that they were just as important as the design of the plane itself.[21] According to Leach and Johnson, those who survive are those who prepare for the worst and have either thought about it or practiced for it.

---

19   https://flightsafety.org/ccs/ccs_mar-apr88.pdf Cabin Crew Safety Vol. 23 No. 2, March/ April 1988.

20   Johnson, Daniel A., Just in Case (New York: Plenum Press, 1984)

21   Excerpt from Time Magazine article entitled "How to Get Out Alive- from hurricanes to 9/11: What the science of evacuation reveals about how humans behave in the worst of times." Written by Amanda Ripley, published Monday April 25, 2005.

A very good friend of mine, and United States Secret Service (USSS) Agent (retired) Mike V., recipient of the USSS Medal of Valor for his heroic actions on the morning of September 11th, 2001, not only survived the attack[22] but helped save the lives of others, due to his first-responder training. Conversely, other survivors of the same event recalled observing their co-workers gather belongings, put on their coats, call loved ones and shut down computers before leaving their offices and cubicles. Per eye witness accounts they "carried on conversations and descended at a leisurely pace" and thus never made it out of the buildings burning down around them. They were neither panicked nor calm, but simply stunned, as an interviewee said; "We were like robots."[23]

You respond to situations like this not because of panic, but because all normalcy has disappeared. Everything you know and are familiar with, is rendered unavailable to your mind. Why would you respond that way?

When you are overloaded with new, unfamiliar and threatening information you enter a state of temporary mental paralysis. This is because your mind must run through several steps to process the new information before your body can react.

---

22   During the terrorist attack on the World Trade Center complex in New York City, NY which killed approximately 3000 people and injured nearly double that number.

23   *Nerve, Poise Under pressure, Serenity Under Stress, and the Brave New Science of Fear and Cool."*, Taylor Clark, Little, Brown and Company, 2011

Per Johnson; cognition, perception, comprehension, decision, implementation and then movement are the steps needed to process new information.[24]

Cognition – the mental action or process of acquiring knowledge and understanding through thought, experience and the senses.[25]

Perception – a method or *mental impression* of that cognition.

Comprehension – the act of understanding that *mental impression.*

Decision – a conclusion or resolution reached after consideration of that *mental impression.*

Implementation – the process of putting that decision into action

Movement – the physical manifestation of that process.

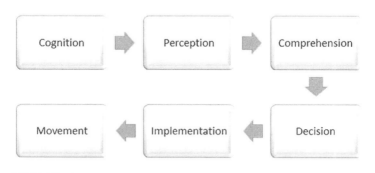

Fig. 2. Six steps to processing information

---

24   *You are not so Smart,* David McRaney, Oneworld, 2012
25   Oxford Dictionary definition, 2012

Leach says that even in the most ideal of circumstances it takes approximately eight to ten seconds to run through this process. That timeline increases dramatically under stress. It takes time to cycle through those six steps. The more time it takes the greater danger you are in.

"In the 1970's psychologist Daniel Johnson found that when he asked subjects to perform a challenging and novel task under high pressure, 45% of them shut down and stopped moving for a minimum of 30 seconds." (Clark)

How can we defeat *Normalcy Bias*? Researchers around the globe continue to search for answers to that very question. Two researchers from the Department of Sociology at Tokyo University; Shunji Mikami and Ken'ichi Ikeda, have done a tremendous amount of research on this subject (human response to disasters) and what can be done to defeat this mental state. The following is information on what Mikami, Ikeda and other researchers have found.

People need information to act. If the information coming at them is new and unfamiliar, if they don't know how or what to do, they cannot act in critical moments. They become "frozen" while trying to process incoming information from their environment. Mikami and Ikeda found that people who survived a disaster had done so by preparing for the worst-case scenario – planning and running drills, running responses, and repetition.

"According to Johnson and Leach, the sort of people who survive are the sort of people who prepare for the worst and practice ahead of time. These people don't deliberate during calamity because they've already done the deliberation the other people around them are just now going through." (McRaney)

People who do not prepare, remain in a state of *Normalcy Bias*. When faced with danger, they enter a state of mental paralysis, becoming frozen. Everything is unfamiliar and the extended time it takes to process incoming information could cost them and their loved ones their lives.

The six steps are a critical factor, and "there is no way to get around this, but you can practice until these steps are no longer complex and thus don't take up valuable brain computation cycles." (Clark)

Practice does not necessarily refer to physical only. Visualization is a mental practice that can be performed without accompanying physical movement. Visualization has been proven to be equally effective as physical practice in reducing the complexity of the six steps, and increasing the speed of familiarization.

> "Noted as one form of mental rehearsal, visualization has been popular since the Soviets started using it back in the 1970s to compete in sports. Now, many athletes employ this technique, including Tiger Woods who has been using it since his pre-teen years. Seasoned athletes use vivid, highly detailed internal images and run-throughs of the entire performance, engaging all their senses in their mental rehearsal, and they combine their knowledge of the sports venue with mental rehearsal. World Champion Golfer, Jack Nicklaus has said: "I never hit a shot, not even in practice, without having

a very sharp in-focus picture of it in my head". Even heavyweight champion, Muhammad Ali, used different mental practices to enhance his performance in the ring such as: "affirmation; visualization; mental rehearsal; self-confirmation; and perhaps the most powerful epigram of personal worth ever uttered: "I am the greatest"".

Brain studies now reveal that thoughts produce the same mental instructions as actions. Mental imagery impacts many cognitive processes in the brain: motor control, attention, perception, planning, and memory. So, the brain is getting trained for actual performance during visualization. It's been found that mental practices can enhance motivation, increase confidence and self-efficacy, improve motor performance, prime your brain for success, and increase states of flow."[26]

Training or running drills and responses, even in thought (visualization), pre-loads information in your conscious and subconscious mind.[27] It creates a familiarity, so the process is no longer complex and cumbersome, which frees your mind from paralysis and allows you to act.

---

26   Excerpt from the article "Seeing Is Believing: The Power of Visualization" by AJ Adams, MAPP https://www.psychologytoday.com/blog/flourish/200912/seeing-is-believing-the-power-visualization

27   International Journal of Mass Emergencies and Disasters, 1985, Human Response to Disasters

Defeating Normalcy Bias

Defeating *Normalcy Bias* increases your chances of surviving an *active threat*. You can defeat this retention device of your most powerful weapon if you:

1. Acknowledge that *Normalcy Bias* exists.
2. Understand how it affects you and that it can be defeated.
3. Stack the deck in your favor with training.

Training includes thinking about what you would do. Playing the "What if" game, and repeating those drills mentally, or physically, compresses the information processing timeline. Even by using your mind's eye - visualization, you can create familiarity, freeing you to act sooner.

Captain Robert Bragg and USSS (retired) Mike V. are real-world examples of how training can help unsheathe your most powerful weapon allowing you to take appropriate action.

Normalcy Bias appears whether you have weeks or months to act like Pompeii (79AD) or Katrina (2005), or only seconds between life and death, like the deadliest event in aviation history (Tenerife) or the worst act of terrorism on US soil (September 11, 2001.)

Even though about 85-90% of us may be subject to the effects of *Normalcy Bias* it *can* be defeated. Knowing what it is, how it works and with minimal training, even a makeshift plan on the fly, you can defeat it. Don't let it get the best of you. In the new normal, your life may one day depend on it.

CHAPTER 2

PERSONAL SECURITY

> "We do not rise to the level of our expectations. We fall to the level of our training."
>
> **ARCHILOCHUS**

You want to feel comfortable yet be protected in the *new normal*. The best way to achieve this is by using your most powerful weapon.

Personal security is exactly what it is – personal. Accepting the *new normal* and defeating *Normalcy Bias* are essential to unsheathing your most powerful weapon. Once unsheathed, how can you use it to ensure your personal security?

Skills and Confidence

If you are a cop, you know that above all, your personal security, and that of your partner are dependent upon your skills and confidence (gained by applied skill). If you are a protective agent, your ability to protect those in your charge is based on these same skills and confidence. The very same holds true if you are concerned about the protection of yourself and your family. The only way to gain skill is by training.

Although we would like to think that we would rise to the occasion, it was the ancient Greek philosopher Archilochus (680-645 BC) who said, "We do not rise to the level of our expectations. We fall to the level of our training."

Importance of Training

Training has been proven integral to the defeat of *Normalcy Bias* and gaining the skills and confidence it takes to survive in the new normal. It was training that helped Captain Bragg work through his *Normalcy Bias*, accurately assess the situation, and do what it took to get the job done. It was training that allowed my US Secret Service Agent brother to save lives during 9/11, and go home to his family when it was over.

The most elite military units in the world know that training is what makes an effective operator. As a federal service provider for NAVSOC[28] it was my job to train US Navy's SEALs in specialized skills. What I took away from that unique experience was that when SEALs are not

---

28   United States Naval Special Operations Command

out on assignment, they are training, and that training is what separates those with the highest skill levels, from those without.

The purpose of training is to gain technical skill and build personal confidence. Skill without confidence is just as ineffective as having confidence but with no skill to back it up. In other words, you don't want your mouth writing checks that your skills can't cash!

Confidence is built by applying your skills repeatedly until they are second nature. An example of this is tying your shoes. Odds are, you're very confident in forming the knot, considering which lace goes first and so forth. You don't really think about it. You just do it, effortlessly.

Skill and confidence – if ever there were a preparatory solution for the new normal it's these two. You build your skills in training, and your confidence in practical application.

In the world of personal security, there are two categories of skills needed by the professionals to keep themselves and their protectee(s)[29] out of harms' way – soft skills and hard skills.

Soft Skills vs Hard Skills

Most people purchase a firearm and keep it in a drawer, a safe, or even carry it concealed. They think of it as a "lucky rabbit's foot that will ward off all evil"[30] in the new normal.

---

29 In protection parlance, a protectee is someone with you that you wish to keep safe from harm.

30 Quote from Clint Smith – Small Arms expert and founder of *Thunder Ranch*

To most shooters carrying concealed, this is the extent of what it takes for protection from a violent physical attack – simply *having* a gun. Other folks may decide to get in shape and buy a gym membership.

The fact of the matter is that physical strength, cardio endurance, guns and the skills to use them, make up only 10% of your overall personal security solution. Your core capability to protect yourself and those with you, are divided into two separate skill sets: *hard skills* and *soft skills*.

Hard skills are your physical capabilities that directly apply to your physically surviving personal combat (i.e. hand-to-hand combat, firearms proficiency, defensive driving). The end-product of physical training - *hard skills* - are gained by development of eye-hand coordination, weapons handling, and marksmanship training. Just like any first-responder, without *hard skills*, you could not effectively respond to a violent physical threat.

Hard skills, by their design, are *reactive*. *Soft skills*, by contrast, are *proactive*.

Utilizing your most powerful weapon, you can be trained to observe, orient, decide and appropriately act to avoid or mitigate an active threat before having no other choice but to defend against it using your *hard skills*.

Soft skills are gained by awareness-based training, to include applying your *situational awareness* and your ability to recognize a threat. Without *soft skills*, you

[professional shooting school]

wouldn't be able to see it coming, and would have no other choice but to rely solely on your *hard skills*.

SKILL	TYPE	USE YOUR	TRAINING	GEAR NEEDED
Hard	Reactive	Hands	Physical	Firearm/ Ammunition/ Knife
Soft	Proactive	Mind	Non-physical	Appropriate Mindset and Situational Awareness

Fig. 3. Soft Skills vs Hard Skills

The balance between *hard skills* and *soft skills* can be illustrated by the example of getting your driver's license. Before you can legally acquire a driver's license, you must pass a test demonstrating your driving knowledge (soft skills) and your physical proficiency (hard skills).

The first part of the test challenges your knowledge of the law, how traffic lights work and other rules of the road. If you pass this part of the test, you are then invited to get behind the wheel and demonstrate your physical skills such as parking, making a three-point turn and the like. You are granted your license only if you pass both the soft skills and hard skills parts of the test.

When it comes to managing an *active threat*, only 10% of managing that threat requires *hard skills*. The initial 90% requires *soft skills*.

Soft Skills	Hard Skills
90%	10%

Fig 4. Skills needed to manage an Active Threat

Your mind is available to you 24/7 and can be trained to ensure your personal security by developing your *soft skills*. Learning these critical skills begins with a working knowledge of interpersonal conflict.

Interpersonal Conflict

The word "aggression" per Merriam-Webster, means "hostile, injurious, or destructive behavior or outlook especially when caused by frustration." The etymology of the word aggression, comes from the ancient Latin *aggredi* which means "to attack."

In modern psychology, human aggression refers to a range of behaviors that can result in both physical and psychological harm to oneself, other people or objects in the environment. This type of social interaction centers on harming another person, either physically or mentally. The expression of aggression can occur in several ways including verbally, mentally and physically.

Physically, human aggression, is a dangerous and harmful form of behavior. Given the new normal, its incidence in social interaction is alarmingly high.

Physical human aggression can be measured on a scale from lowest to highest intensity. This is referred to as the *Scale of Human Aggression*. At its mildest physical expression, human aggression can be categorized by what is commonly called a *scuffle*.

Triggered by verbal insults, challenges, or similar combination of confrontational communication; a scuffle sits at the bottom of the *Scale of Human Aggression*. You may likely observe this physical expression in the form of finger-pointing, grabbing of collars, shoving or pushing.

Usually accompanied by shouting or emotionally charged language, it is often attributed to the resulting impulse of motivated frustration and usually dissipates as quickly as it ignites. A scuffle is generally squelched by those nearby or even by the perpetrators themselves unwilling to take it to the next level. Other than a bruised ego, there is very little or no bodily injury resulting from a scuffle.

The next step up from a scuffle is a *fight*. The iconic barroom brawl, two kids fighting after school or a fight between players during a game, represent typical examples of this mid-level physical expression of human aggression. The purpose of the quintessential fight is to determine dominance - who is the alpha. A fight can result in physical injury ranging from a minor injury to waking up in an intensive care unit two days later.

Topping off the very highest Scale of Human Aggression is *personal combat*.

Here you are literally fighting for your life. Usually involving weapons such as guns or knives, they are trying to kill you and it is either you or him/ them. Only the victor survives.

Although few people will ever encounter extreme physical violence in their lifetime, there are some truly bad people out there, who kill other human beings for a paycheck, street creds, or just for fun. These are the likes of war-hardened terrorists, religious extremists, hardened convicts, inner-city gangs and the criminally insane. We are merely tourists in their world.

Far more intense than a *scuffle* or a *fight*, *personal combat* minimally results in one or more combatants landing in intensive care with a very high probability of death or permanent bodily injury. When it comes to personal security, your greatest physical risk is that raised in *personal combat*.

Delineating these three levels of human aggression, is the resulting level of personal injury sustained by each, and referred to as, the *Scale of Injury*.

Scale of Injury

Anywhere on the Scale of Human Aggression, when things get physical, injury becomes a significant factor. Applying your most powerful weapon to any level of human aggression, it is imperative to base your decisions on what will keep your bodily injuries, and that of those with you, to a bare minimum.

In any physical attack, there exists the potential for five levels of injury referred to as the *Scale of Injury*. At the lowest end of the scale is Level 0 or *no injury*, which is the most desirable outcome in any scrape. Level 0 or no injury on the *Scale of Injury*, means you walked away from a scuffle or even a fight with not a scratch or bruise on your body. This is the very best possible outcome of any physical violence. The next level up from *no injury* is

Level 1 or a *minor injury* such as bruises, scratches, minor cuts, or abrasions. Having experienced bruises, paper-cuts and the like, we've all worn a Band-Aid© at one time or another since we were kids.

Minor injuries are uncomfortable and inconvenient, but still better than the next level up on the scale, which is a Level 2 or *recoverable injury* such as a broken leg, broken arm, broken nose, and the like. Although debilitating and requiring significant convalescence, you can recover from these and live to tell others about the story behind your scars.

Up one more rung on the Scale of Injury is Level 3 describing a *permanent injury* which would include such horrific results as blindness, paralysis, or maiming for life. Unlike a recoverable injury, sustaining a Level 3 injury is an impaired condition by which you would be encumbered for the remainder of your life.

The last and final step in the Scale of Injury is Level 4 a *fatal injury*—death, from which there is no recovery. This is your worst case possible scenario.

Injuries are a tactical consideration. When making the decision to take physical action, you must consider that anything above Level 1 renders you combat ineffective and makes you a detriment to yourself and to those for whom you may be responsible. The secret to prevailing at any level of human aggression, is to keep your *Scale of Injury*, and that of those with you, to a bare minimum.

Using the scale to your advantage means making any tactical decisions based on where the outcome of those decisions may place you and/ or your protectee(s) on that scale.

In the new normal, you may find yourself up against an assailant(s) using any high-tech or low-tech weapon or implement capable of causing physical damage. There are two categories of weapons that can raise your *Scale of Injury*. One category is ballistic weapons: describing explosive devices and firearms, which can include a rifle, shotgun, or handgun.

Fig 5. The Scale of Injury

The other is non-ballistic weapons which can include: edged weapons (knife, broken glass, screw driver, etc.,) that may be used to slash open flesh and major arteries, or puncture vital organs. They may also include impact weapons (baton, baseball bat, tire iron, golf club, etc.,) which can be used to crush your skull and bones.

Flexible weapons (rope, chain, bungee, etc.,) are another example of non-ballistic weapons. When fixed tightly around your neck like a garrote, can be used to either asphyxiate you or break your neck. The best example of flexible weapon use in history, was the primary method of execution in the United States up until 1938, which was hanging.

A non-ballistic weapon in the hands of a skilled or deter-mined assailant can raise your scale of injury up to a Level 4. Personal weapons such as closed fists, elbows, knees and shins can be used to punch, kick, and otherwise cause extensive bodily damage raising your *Scale of Injury.* Max Baer[31], a Great Depression era boxer, beat an opponent so badly with his fists, that he eventually died from his injuries.[32]

As in the cases of London Bridge[33], Ohio State University[34] and Berlin, Germany[35] you may find yourself confront-

---

31   Heavyweight boxing champion Maximilian Adelbert "Max" Baer (February 11, 1909 – November 21, 1959) was an American boxer of the 1930s.

32   Boxer Frankie Campbell died following his knockout loss to Baer. Years later, Ernie Schaef died following his defeat to Primo Carnera, allegedly it was Ernie's savage beating at the hands of Max Baer only a few months before which resulted in his death.

33   June 3, 2017, 8 people were killed and 48 wounded in an attack that took place in the *Southwark* district of London, England, when three men drove a van into pedestrians on London Bridge. Wielding knives, the men then left the van and went to the nearby Borough Market area, where they stabbed people in and around restaurants and pubs

34   November 28, 2016, a terrorist vehicle-ramming and stabbing attack occurred at 9:52 a.m. EST at Ohio State University in Columbus, Ohio. 13 people were hospitalized for injuries.

35   Terrorist attack on 19 December 2016, a truck was deliberately driven into a Christmas market at Breitscheidplatz in Berlin, Germany which left 12 people dead and 56 injured.

ing an incoming vehicle and attackers armed with knives which are considered low-tech, non-ballistic weapons.

While delivering a train-the-trainer class at a federal agency in Quantico, Virginia, I was prompted with a question referencing avoiding the *Scale of Human Aggression* and keeping your *Scale of Injury* low. A student-instructor asked me "Sir, what is the one thing we can teach our students that will *guarantee* their personal security no matter what the circumstances?"

The answer was, and still is; there is no silver bullet. Same as there is no one-word answer to physical violence, there is no one guaranteed technique that will work every single time. If there was, then we would all know it and you would never see or hear anything in the news about people getting killed or injured because of an *active threat*.

However, personal security can be made easy. We do know that training, which builds skill and confidence, is the very best solution in the new normal. It will help you defeat *Normalcy Bias* and is paramount to developing your most powerful weapon.

CHAPTER 3

YOUR MOST POWERFUL WEAPON

"Nothing can stop the man with the right mental attitude from achieving his goal; nothing on earth can help the man with the wrong mental attitude."

THOMAS JEFFERSON

To be effective, a weapon must be sturdy, well-built and reliable. It should be so reliable that you would trust your life to it. Deep in the shadows of the defense intelligence community, there may be, hypothetically-speaking, certain unarmed clandestine service officers who risk life and limb in performance of their job responsibilities in high-threat or non-permissive environments.

Armed with only their training and confidence, they must, hypothetically-speaking, navigate through hostile and demanding circumstances. They need to remain calm and collected in situations of extreme duress, and must have what it takes mentally, to successfully apply their *soft skills*. What allows them to keep so cool under pressure, that you can add to *your* arsenal?

1. Mindset
2. Mental Toughness
3. Being a Hard Target
4. Taking Control

Mindset

The primary component in using your most powerful weapon is choosing the one that will best serve you. There are two most common mindsets. The first is, "It will never happen to me." How often have you heard this before or know of someone who thinks that way? If you ever watch a documentary where they interview survivors of tragic experiences, the two most common statements you will usually hear are: "I couldn't believe how fast it happened" and "I couldn't believe it was happening to me."

The second is, "Someone else will handle it." Many people think that the cavalry, somehow notified, will ride over the horizon to save their day, and that all they need to do is wait for its arrival. Nothing could be further from the truth.

A third mindset, separate from and opposite these first two, and the one you rarely run into, is "Personal security is my responsibility." Of the three, which one do you think will serve you best?

Choosing the most effective mindset is not a matter of reading a book, attending a seminar or watching a video. It is simply a matter of making up your mind. All you need to do is make the conscious decision that personal security is *your* responsibility and adopt that decision internally. Only after adopting this mindset, you must visualize using your most powerful weapon as wielding a mental sword. If you plan on using that sword – especially in personal combat, it must be tempered, hardened and ready for crushing impact. In plain speak, you need to be mentally tougher than your adversaries – the second component in using your most powerful weapon.

Mental Toughness

As a personal security instructor, I am often asked, "If it does hit the fan, and I find myself staring at the white elephant, how would I control my anxiety?" The answer is to develop an inner strength that resides somewhere in the depth of your being, affording you the confidence to overcome anxiety. A protection industry term for this inner strength is *mental toughness*. Mental toughness is a subject that can be studied, cultivated and developed through training and practice.

Mental toughness is a measure of individual resilience and confidence that can predict success at work, in competition and under extreme pressure. It refers to any set of positive non-physical attributes that helps you to cope with and perform under duress and in difficult situations.

Throughout history, the likes of the ancient Roman and Spartan armies, because of their unparalleled discipline, training and mental toughness in physical combat, commanded unequivocal respect from their enemies.

Fast forward to today. Over the past three decades I have trained some of the most elite special forces operators in existence. They are the toughest, hardest, and the most highly respected of the Special Operation Forces (SOF) community on the planet. Akin to their ancient Roman and Spartan predecessors, they have something useful to teach us about inner strength and performance under duress.

As was explained to me, by those who made the grade, anybody in shape can do push-ups, run an obstacle course, etc., but not everyone can try out for a special operations unit. Only those who have the right frame of mind can accomplish this task. Even if somehow you pass the initial try-out phase, the next level up is *selection* phase during which you are driven to the very edge of breaking.

The same holds true for Olympic athletes pushed to their very limits. At that extreme level, there's only one thing that separates those who quit from those who don't quit, and that is *mental toughness*.

Outside the military and Olympics, there are survivors of brutal life-taking events such as airplane, train or bus crashes you hear about where other people perished yet *they* somehow made it out alive. What's the one common denominator shared by these extraordinary survivors? What separates the entrepreneurs of that one successful startup business from the multitude of com-petitors that failed? They all share one thing in common – *mental toughness*.

What exactly is *mental toughness*? If you ask an elite athlete, mental toughness is the ability to remain focused and perform well under stressful circumstances. If you ask an elite warrior, mental toughness is the ability to remain calm in extremely dangerous, or life-threatening situations, and make the appropriate decisions and task performances to ensure mission success. If you ask one of those life-and-death incident survivors who escaped the impossible, they will tell you it was their resiliency and pure will that drove them on.

In her *New York Times* bestseller, Grit: The Power of Passion and Perseverance, psychologist Angela Duckworth drawing from her research and interviews of cadets struggling through their first days at West Point, teachers working in some of the toughest schools, dozens of high-level achievers from JP Morgan CEO Jamie Dimon, to New Yorker cartoon editor Bob Mankoff, to Seattle Seahawks Coach Pete Carroll, demonstrates anyone striving to succeed, (i.e. parents, students, educators, athletes, or business people), that the secret to success is not talent but a but a unique combination of passion and long-term perseverance. This is what she calls "Grit" and what protection professionals call *Mental Toughness*.

If you want to cash in on the secret of what it takes to be part of SOF, win an Olympic gold medal, build and run a successful business or be prepared for an active threat, then you need this same *mental toughness*. How do you get it? It comes from three very personal and internal sources: heart (passion), will (perseverance) and strength (resilience).

Heart or passion, is an intense and overpowering feeling or conviction that provides the driving force behind your intentions. You hear this all the time about a stellar athlete who is passionate about her sport or a great musician who is passionate about his music. The same passion can apply to a relationship or a job or a life's calling. Being passionate about something is about being motivated. The greater the passion, the greater the motivation to do something about it.

Having the heart to face any challenge is something you are either born with or can develop. When teaching a civilian weapons self-defense course, there are many times when a soccer mom who is taking the class, although concerned about her security and that of her family, pulls me off to the side during a break and confides in me "I love the training and I'm really learning a lot, but I honestly don't think I could actually use this against another person." My first response to her is "What if that same person was trying to hurt your kids?" She instantly kicks into mama bear and says "Well, that's different! I would do *whatever* it takes to stop them!" She found her passion. Because of her newfound motivation, she works diligently on building her skills and confidence for the remainder of the program.

The first of three qualities comprising *mental toughness*, heart or passion, is the raw material from which mental toughness is forged. It is your motivation. You either have it (born with or developed) or you don't.

Just by the fact that you're reading this proves that you have the heart or passion and are motivated to protect your family and your loved ones from bad things that happen to good people. If you couldn't care less about yours or their personal security, then there's no motivation. Without motivation, there is no action. Only the motivated act.

You're off to a *very* good start as passion affords you the motivation to usher yourself and your family through an *active threat*. You can put a checkmark in the "Has Heart" box and rest assured that you're a third the way there, on the path to achieving *mental toughness.*

The second of these qualities is having the will or perseverance to succeed. The Merriam-Webster dictionary definition of perseverance is "continued effort to do or achieve something despite difficulties, failure, or opposition." Perseverance is the hammer that forges mental toughness. America's first billionaire oil industry magnate John D. Rockefeller (1839 –1937), once said "I do not think that there is any other quality so essential to success of any kind as the quality of perseverance." In plain speak, perseverance is the will to keep going.

The term "indominable will" can be traced to the 6th century BCE Military general and strategist Sun Tzu's and his renowned treatise on combat The Art of War which is still used today as a reference to the importance of indomitable will. Napoleon Bonaparte and General Douglas MacArthur are claimed to have drawn inspiration from it. Beyond the world of war, business and management gurus have also applied Sun Tzu's ideas to office politics and corporate strategy.

Mahatma Gandhi said "Strength does not come from physical capacity. It comes from an indomitable will." A full-body workout for the mind allows us to apply that strength to other activities, and to solve problems more effectively and creatively in both academic and social settings. Despite opposition, failure, or difficulty, the more they try to pin you down, the more you use your will to press on. The ancient Greeks trained their warrior class to relish those life's moments when they were faced with adversity because these were the hammer strikes that helped forge their will. Next time you find yourself in a difficult personal situation, be like the ancient Greek warrior who has been offered the golden opportunity to further strengthen his will.

When you use your will to face any challenge, regardless of how big or how small, just like building muscle from weightlifting, it strengthens your resolve. Perseverance translates to having an unshakable will to get through it no matter what the circumstances.

The third and equally important component of mental toughness is mental strength or resiliency. Resiliency is the mental capacity to recover quickly from difficulties. It is the temper of mental toughness. Bouncing back when things get ugly gives you confidence which, in turn, makes you stronger.

Get comfortable being uncomfortable.[36] You cannot get stronger if you never leave your comfort zone. Learning to be comfortable with uncomfortable situations will force you to learn from the situation instead of escaping from it.

---

36   https://lifehacker.com/get-comfortable-being-uncomfortable-1599385696

Health coaches, such as Maria Bogdanos at PsychCentral. com, offer positive steps to building emotional resiliency that you can follow when you put yourself in such uncomfortable situations.[37] Use critical thinking, reasoning and problem-solving techniques on your own so you will trust your instincts more. Resist the urge to blame others. Also resist the urge to expect too much from them. You are creative and resourceful enough to find ways that work best for how you are wired.

We are prone to stay inside the boundaries of what we consider our comfort zone. Once pushed outside those boundaries, beyond the perimeter we have earned that real-estate, and the right to be comfortable in it. Building up your resiliency occurs each time you step outside your comfort zone. Next chance you get to step out into the unknown or unfamiliar, don't pass up the opportunity to further develop your mental strength.

One of the most prominent contemporary examples of mental toughness is that of First Sergeant Kasal. In a firefight with insurgents in a house in Fallujah, although wounded by seven 7.62×39mm rounds and hit by more than 43 pieces of hot fragmentation from a grenade while using his body to shield an injured fellow Marine, First Sergeant Kasal refused to quit fighting and was able to return fire with a handgun, killing at least one insurgent. Kasal is credited with saving the lives of several Marines during the U.S. assault on insurgent strongholds in Fallujah in November 2004. By the time he was carried

---

37   https://psychcentral.com/blog/archives/2013/10/26/5-steps-to-help-build-emotional-resilience/

out of the house by LCpl Chris Marquez and LCpl Dan Shaffer, then-First Sergeant Kasal had lost approximately 60 percent of his blood. Blood-soaked and still holding his M9 pistol and KA-Bar fighting knife he was helped from the building by fellow Marines.

In contrast to a powderpuff world afflicted by political correctness, micro aggressions and safe spaces, cultivating mental strength or resilience provides you a tremendous advantage. By developing the ability to stick it out, as those around you fold like lawn chairs, you set yourself up for success.

Rome was not built in a day. Similarly, developing *mental toughness* is a journey, not a destination. If you haven't already, then ignite your passion. Stoke your heart fire by focusing on the thought that your life and the lives of your family are dependent upon your motivation. Build your will. Choose to be like the ancient Greek warriors. Instead of dreading your next personal challenge, embrace it. Know as they did, that it is a gift and opportunity to strengthen your indomitable spirit. Yours is the will to make it through *no matter what* they throw at you. Remaining flexible in your resiliency ensures that when you get knocked you will get back up. Step outside your comfort zone and use that opportunity like a workout at the gym to build your mental strength.

Yes, it's true that none of us is exempt from the possibility of being involved in an active threat, but that doesn't mean you should be worried about it. *Mental toughness* affords you the personal freedom to get through anything without fear of failure. It provides assurance that no matter what, you will land on your feet.

Mental toughness is your mind's armor that glances away incoming blows, not only the ones that come in from the outside, but especially the most insidious – thoughts of self-doubt, or other self-sabotaging machinations that may emerge from within. Mental toughness brings you comfort in knowing what was once something you didn't think you could handle, is now well within your grasp.

Mental toughness is an enduring quality that keeps you strong, confident and focused even in the face of adversity. Heart, your passion and motivation, combined with will, your indomitable spirit, and mental strength, your resiliency, are the kernels of mental toughness. In today's new normal, mental toughness isn't a luxury, it's a necessity.

Be a Hard Target

The next, and equally important, component in using your most powerful weapon, is to be a hard target. Derived from Colonel Cooper's[38] classic mindset lectures, we are afforded the opportunity of one-stop-shopping for this most coveted component in the defense intelligence community.

According to Colonel Cooper, to become a determined or dedicated hard target, you must:

1. Accept the fact - that bad things happen and could happen *today, n*ot some far off distant future time but right here and right now or in the next few moments.
2. Have the willingness - to take action against a specific person or persons.
3. Have a plan – and the decision that will cause you to execute that plan.

Starting with "Accept the fact", there isn't one active military or law enforcement professional worth their salt, whose job it is to protect others for a living, that doesn't recite the mantra "Bad things happen and they could happen to me today, maybe in the next few seconds," when they step into their work environment. Just by accepting this fact of life, here in the new normal, gives you a leg up and directs your perspective toward preparedness.

---

38   John Dean "Jeff" Cooper (May 10, 1920 – September 25, 2006) was a United States Marine, the creator of the "modern technique" of handgun shooting, an expert on personal defense, and the use and history of small arms. He was one of my most prolific and influential instructors.

The second, "having the willingness," is using the will of your mental toughness to act against a specific person or persons. Best described by the unassuming wife of a senior executive who had hired me to run a residential security assessment, Ms. Jones had no military or law enforcement background whatsoever. She had the toughest job on the planet – raising three kids.

She told me that if she was in a parking lot and confronted by an assailant coming after her or the kids, that even with the three kids in the car, buckled in of course, she would smash into him with their minivan pinning him to the parking garage wall like a bug. She certainly had the intention to do whatever it took to protect her children and that intention was reflected in her willingness to take action against a physical threat. There was no doubt in my mind that Ms. Jones possessed mental toughness.

Later in the interview I asked her to describe how she moved with the kids from a controlled area (shopping mall, airport, etc.,) to the family car and conducted the loading and unloading of everyone in and out of the vehicle. She went on to explain a plan of action and protective movement that would bring a tear of joy to any unit commander. She was the most tactically sound soccer mom I'd ever met in my entire career!

Lastly, *have a plan and make the decision that will cause you to execute that plan*, is best illustrated by example. My favorite tactical soccer mom relayed yet another story where she was out shopping with the kids and observed some "creepy guy" (her words) checking her out from across the store. As she completed her payment at the register she made the decision that if that same guy was still hanging around after she checked out, then she was going to ask the manager to walk her and the kids out to the car. She had a plan and made the proactive decision that would cause her to execute that plan if the threat presented itself.

To convert yourself from a soft target to a hard target, all you need to do is:

1. Accept the fact (it could happen at any moment)
2. Have the will to act
3. Have a plan that you will execute based on your decision to act

Being a hard target is to, every once in a while, recite the "any moment" mantra internally, remind yourself that it could hit the fan in the blink of an eye. Know that you have the willingness to do what it takes to solve the problem, should the situation arise and that you will act based on your plan.

Actions speak louder than words in the new normal. Think like a hard target, act like a hard target, and you will be a hard target.

Take Control

The last, but certainly not the least component in using your most powerful weapon, is to take control. Whether you accept it or not, we live in a world that demands either you control the threat, or the threat controls you. The supply for that demand is knowing how to take and keep control of an *active threat*.

When an employee of CIA, it was my responsibility to support the protection of global US assets including infrastructure and personnel. My activities might include everything from sitting in front of a laptop at Langley, to boots on the ground in a war zone. In support of these efforts was the need for personal security training that worked in high-threat areas to keep people and operations safe from active threats.

It is this fundamental training, presented in four (4) parts:

1. How to Control Your Environment (Part I)
2. How to Control a Threat (Part II)
3. How to Defeat an Attack (Part III)
4. How to Control Fear (Part IV)

that will build your skills and confidence. Representing ninety percent of your personal security solution, these are the critical *soft skills* that you may never need. However, should you need them, they *do* work in war zones and they *will* work for you against an active threat.

PART I

HOW TO CONTROL YOUR ENVIRONMENT

CHAPTER 4

SITUATIONAL AWARENESS

"It's not what you look at that matters, it's what you see."
HENRY DAVID THOREAU

Situational Awareness is the ability to observe, identify, process, and comprehend the critical elements of information about your immediate environment. Simply put, it's *really* knowing what's going on around you. Personal security is 90% situational awareness.

On an assignment, once I was driving way out in the boonies in the middle of nowhere in which I was tasked with delivering a package to a secure facility. Driving along a long and dusty road I pulled up next to a single-person guard shack with a very tall and large muscular female guard in full uniform wearing dark sunglasses, a guard's hat and a gun. She stared down from the little guard shack window in silence at me, with no facial expression whatsoever.

The usual drill was to show the nice armed guard in the tower your color-coded key-card. As I didn't know which card was a match for this facility, I fumbled though my small stack and I showed her the green one, but no response. Then I flashed the red one, no response. Then I flashed the yellow one, and again, no response. Finally, she couldn't take it anymore, and pointed down to the giant three-foot tall diamond-shaped florescent yellow sign that read "Present Driver's License to Guard." It couldn't have been more in my face. In fact, I had to look over it to see the guard! I was looking right at it and didn't see it. There I was a trained observer – your tax dollars hard at work.

Using this embarrassing moment to illustrate an important point, how many times have you looked directly at your watch but failed to see what time it was and then needed to look again? How about driving home looking directly at the road signs and blowing right past yours? Why? Because you were not present. Your eyes were physically looking, but you weren't there and didn't see what you were looking at. A famous quote applies by Henry David Thoreau "It's not what you look at that matters, it's what you see." How can you see what you're looking at? By using *Situational Awareness*.

Most have either heard the term or know what *Situational Awareness* is, but how can it be used to control your environment? The short answer is twofold:

1. Apply Your Awareness
2. Recognize a Threat

Apply Your Awareness

Yet another contribution to the world of personal security made by Colonel Cooper, is what he called the awareness "Color Codes" which is the first component of using our *Situational Awareness* to control your environment.

Developed by Cooper back in the 1960's, there are four conditions of awareness applied to environmental observation, and were adopted by the US Defense, Intelligence and law enforcement communities. You can think of these as settings on your "personal security radar," where you can click your dial up or down to any one of the four as needed. The lowest setting is *Condition White* which offers the least volume of awareness. Sometimes called "home mode," this setting describes when you're sitting comfortably at home in front of your TV with doors locked, perfectly safe and in a completely controlled environment replete with locks, alarms, cameras, firewalls, etc.

Your home is your castle, your sanctuary and *Condition White (Home Mode)* is perfectly applicable at home. However, the second you pop your head outside your front door, it's time to click your radar up to the next level of awareness known as *Condition Yellow* or "public mode." Leaving your radar setting down at condition white when out in public makes you a soft target.

Seasoned intelligence, military and law enforcement operators accept the fact that we live in the new normal and, realizing that it could happen at any time, keep their radar setting at condition yellow. It's important to know this is not paranoia, but that you have only two choices when you're in public: being prepared and aware of your surroundings aka *Condition Yellow*, or being unprepared and unaware of your surroundings.

Paranoia sits at one end of the spectrum and preparedness at the extreme opposite end. You don't want to spoil fun and adventure, but at the same time, you want to do everything you can to not be made vulnerable.

If you happen to observe a potential threat you are placed on mental alert and click up an awareness notch on your personal security radar. Here, you apply *Condition Orange*, which means that you have identified a specific threat. A good example of this is Ms. Jones who spotted that creepy guy at the grocery store. She had switched up to condition orange.

Condition Orange (Alert Mode), indicates that you should be willing and prepared to take action against that specific threat.

The highest setting on your radar is *Condition Red*. It means that you are in the fight now. As things have now gone physical, you are called to action (*Action Mode*). There is no turning back here. You must now make good on that plan and decision which caused you to act.

Knowing that you have a personal security radar setting and that you can click it up or down depending on what you observe. It allows you to apply your awareness to your environment. Using the color codes certainly helps make you a hard target, but what should you look for so that you know *when* to click it up or down?

When at airports or train stations and the like, you often hear the cliché "See it report it." But what exactly is "it"? The answer is: the development of an active threat. Being able to identify a threat, using your situational awareness, is what affords you the opportunity to control that threat.

Threat Recognition

The next component of using your *situational awareness* to control your environment is how to recognize a threat or *Threat Recognition.*

Proactively identifying threats requires first adopting the appropriate mindset (personal security is *my* responsibility), applying your *situational awareness* (personal security radar) to your environment, and your ability to recognize a threat. Once a threat has been identified, this information can then be used to determine your best course of action.

To identify a threat, you must be able to read your environment, which includes events, objects and the people around you, and glean relevant information to determine if there may be something potentially harmful to you.

Regardless of your background, gender, political affiliation or personal belief, at birth you were equipped with the certain organic tools to help you read your immediate environment to detect or identify a threat.

This equipment includes:

1. Your five senses – sight, sound, touch, taste and smell
2. Your sixth sense – intuitive hit or gut feeling
3. Your primal instinct – sense of self-preservation

How can you use these organic tools and further develop them into valuable threat recognition soft skills?

Your Five Senses

Using your eyes, you can observe people and events around you. You can see body language, cues, nonverbal signals, and vignettes or scenarios unfolding such as a couple arguing or a mom scolding her kids.

You can use your ears to listen for screeching tires, explosions, gunfire or people screaming. You can use your nose to detect smoke, gas or other potentially dangerous odors. You can feel the change in temperature with your skin such as standing next to fire or pressure from a blast percussion. You can taste ash, pepper spray or other airborne particles.

Data Points

Your five senses can be used as finely tuned environmental sensors to identify and deliver multiple data points to your awareness for processing. It's what street savvy cops call "tells". For example, "Officer Smith just knew the gang-banger was carrying a firearm" because he could see him adjust his gait a certain way, favor one side over the other, look uncomfortable when standing on one side of his body, kept fidgeting on that same side, etc.,

Given this valuable incoming information you can formulate an immediate response to your environment that could possibly save your life. Case and point is an event which occurred during a 1998 attack on the US embassy in Nairobi, Kenya, Africa.[39]

A military spouse and mother of two young girls, was at the U.S. embassy Nairobi, Kenya that day with several other people. She was working in an indoor office by one of those old fashioned heavy steel work desks. Having no military or law enforcement background, she paid close attention to the words of her concerned husband. He had a tremendous military background and imparted to her the difference between cover and concealment. He further advised that if she were to hear gunfire, no matter where she was, or what she was doing to take cover. On that fateful day, when gunfire erupted, heeding her husband's sound tactical advice, she slipped under the desk using it as cover. She was knocked unconscious by an explosion that followed the gunfire. She awoke shortly thereafter shaken, but with no debilitating injuries only to find her co-workers either killed or severely injured by the same blast. Using her situational awareness, and acting on her sensory input, she clearly identified the active threat and moved to cover.

Allow yourself to receive the incoming information from your five senses, and take that tenth of a second to process it, to determine what's going on. Was that gunfire? Which

---

39   The 1998 United States embassy bombings were attacks that occurred on August 7, 1998, in which over 200 people were killed in nearly simultaneous truck bomb explosions in two East African cities, one at the U.S. Embassy in Dar es Salaam, Tanzania, the other at the U.S. Embassy in Nairobi, Kenya.

direction is it coming from? Acquired by your five senses, incoming information can be grouped into two categories: *Event Indicators* and *Threat Indicators*.

Event indicators are those activities which you can observe that are visual or audio cues as to what's going to happen next in your environment. For example, in traffic, if you observe someone pull their foot off the brake pedal and move it toward the gas pedal, this is a visual indicator that the car is about to move faster. If someone moves their hand toward a doorknob it is a visual indicator that the door is about to open.

We see thousands of similar event indicators every day. However, when an *Event Indicator* gets your attention and makes the hair on the back of your neck stand up, such as a closed fist, or someone getting into your space, giving you the social finger or the hairy eyeball, the smell of smoke, or the sound of gunfire, then it is called a *Threat Indicator*.

Threat Indicators

Bad things don't happen to good people out of the blue. They are a gradual progression of human aggression and pre-cursors to violence. The key to preventing a potential threat from progressing into an active threat is to first identify *threat indicators*.

Such indicators are often your only visible clues or observable pre-attack behaviors that something bad is about to happen. Although, they may sometimes be subtle, these observations can provide enough information for you to orient to your surroundings, make your decision based on updated information and then act on that decision.

Referencing the 1998 US Embassy Nairobi incident, when that young lady heard gunfire, she identified that incoming sensory information as a *threat indicator*. As such, this prompted her to take cover. The other employees, when they heard gunfire, did not identify it as an actionable *threat indicator*, and instead went to the window to see what the commotion was all about. Fully exposed to the threat, when the ensuing explosives were detonated, all of them were hit with shrapnel, not all of them survived.

Your Sixth Sense

Some people call it a sixth sense or a gut feeling. Sometimes called a premonition or intuitive hit, it is where you "just know" that something isn't quite right. It's the most fine-tuned of the early-warning tools you have on board, and something you cannot afford to ignore.

In his landmark book, *The Gift of Fear*, author Gavin de Becker wrote that fear is a gift and that you intuitively know when you are in danger or that something bad is about to happen to you. He presented that there are many cues that we do not openly perceive that tell you that you're in trouble. Many times, you ignore these cues. He told the story of a woman who noticed a man walking up in her rear-view mirror and ignored it right before she was accosted. He said if you could somehow make yourself attune to the cues announcing that you are in danger, you would be safer, and that is a gift, thus the title. He went on to further discuss how intuition provides a series of cues that are often not readily perceived or ignored.

In his best-selling book, *Blink*, about the intuitive parts of decision-making, Malcolm Gladwell presents a concept he calls "thin-slicing." He presents there can be "as much value in the blink of an eye than in months of rational analysis." He encourages his readers to not push aside their first thought in favor of getting more information in deciding. Some people are more intuitive which doesn't necessarily go hand-in-hand with intelligence or access to more information.

In support of Gladwell and de Becker, there are numerous reports from the field of medicine where experienced care-givers simply "just knew" what was wrong with a patient. The ancient Gnostics[40] called this "knowing by knowing."

Think of a time when, without using your eyes, you just knew that someone was looking at you from across a room or from a car stopped next to you at a red traffic light. When you looked in that direction, you confirmed it to be true. Or the time when you were just thinking about someone you hadn't had any contact with for a very long time who suddenly called you out of the blue. It is these intuitive hits that can also provide you with the earliest possible warning of imminent danger and should *not* be ignored.

---

40   A modern construction of the archaic Greek term *Gnosis* referencing knowledge based on personal experience or perception.

A Woman's Intuition

Women have a more heightened or attuned intuition than men, but do not often use it to their advantage. Ignoring that intuitive hit can get you in big trouble. In one case, a female clerk was closing a clothing store late at night and was in the process of locking the shop door when a man placed his hand on the door that she had just locked. He explained, through the glass, that it was his wife's birthday, and he had to bring her a gift.

The clerk's intuition was screaming to her that there was something not right about this guy. However, she thought to herself "Oh, don't be so silly, this poor man is out tonight trying to find a gift for his wife! How could I be so paranoid as to not help him?", she completely disregarded what her intuition was telling her and let him into the store. A few hours later she was found beaten nearly to death behind a sales counter by law enforcement, at the hands of the very same "poor man."

In a separate incident, a woman was about to step on to an elevator going up to her office on the 24th floor to retrieve something late at night that she had left at work earlier that day, when a man stepped up to get onto the elevator with her. She was immediately alerted by a feeling that warned her to not get on the elevator with this guy.

Instead of heeding that admonition, she stepped onto the elevator with the man. He asked her which floor and she replied, "Twenty-four please." He pressed the 24th floor button, but no another. Observing this, her inner voice piped up again and shouted at her to get away from him as quickly as possible. Ignoring the warning a second time, she thought to herself "Don't be so rude! He's dressed in a suit and looks like a businessman. There's nothing to worry about!" She found herself filing a police report later that night after being beaten and raped in her own office.

Although used by the experts and works when applied, clicking your personal security radar up and down according to your environment, is only one tool in your kit. If you get a blip *anywhere* on your radar screen, regardless of *how* it gets there, that's all the alert you need to determine if it is an actionable item.

Threat Indicators can be anything unusual – things you wouldn't expect to see or sense, such as threatening body language, or nonverbal signals, a behavior that piques your interest, or that feeling of danger. If something just isn't right, seems out of place, if doesn't look right or doesn't feel right, then it's probably not right!

Take full advantage of any opportunity that helps you to proactively determine what is out of place. Any *threat indicator* could quickly lead to more *threat indicators*. Like a pot of water set on the stove about to boil over, if things start to go bad, they will continue to go bad and quickly accelerate. This is exactly the reason why you need to act the split second you identify them.

Primal Instincts

At our primal core, we alert to life-threatening danger. This instinct acts as a motivator in self-preservation. In addition to observing your environment with your five senses and your sixth sense, you can use this motivator to help you spot those things to which you should be alerted, such as an anomaly.

Spot an Anomaly

Integral to *Threat Recognition* is spotting an anomaly. The Webster's dictionary definition of an anomaly is "something that deviates from what is standard, normal, or expected." An anomaly can be an oddity, peculiarity, abnormality, irregularity, inconsistency, or incongruity. You can align your most powerful weapon with your primal instincts to help you detect anomalies by knowing how to read a baseline and acknowledge a change in baseline rhythm.

Use Your Baseline

Read Your Baseline

In the world of personal security, experience teaches that when something isn't normal, then stand by and brace for impact. The U.S. intelligence community is trained to observe things that appear to be out of place. How we know that they are out of place is by first establishing, and then reading, a "baseline."

To do this, determine what it is you expect to observe or experience in your immediate environment. Next look for *event indicators* that fall outside or vary from those expectations. Should you perceive such indicators, they may be considered potential *threat indicators*.

You walk into a quiet coffee shop. You order your coffee, you sit down and scan the room while waiting for your order to come up. Looking around you observe a few business people, a couple of students, an elderly couple, all experiencing a relatively quiet atmosphere. You notice some folks are in conversation, while others are typing away on their laptop or cell phone. Elevator music is playing in the background and the vibe is mellow. Consciously or subconsciously you establish a baseline for all these *event indicators* that you consider to be normal for your immediate environment.

Suddenly, a guy walks in with his hands in his coat pockets sweating profusely. You notice he seems nervous or agitated and keeps looking back and forth at the cash register and the security cameras. His body language and non-verbal signs are *event indicators* that are present that shouldn't be there – or what we call above the baseline and may be considered *threat indicators*.

The opposite of this is; you look behind the serving counter where you expect to see baristas and even though you've been waiting your turn to order for more than fifteen minutes there is nobody behind the counter. You glance behind the windows of the swinging aluminum doors in the back and still you see nobody. If you expect something to be there and it isn't – or what we call below the baseline, these missing items may be considered *threat indicators*.

Baseline Rhythm

Another way to effectively use your baseline is to set a baseline for your environment and then allow yourself to "feel the rhythm" of that baseline.

68

Hailing from the world of professional protection, with a little practice, you can sense when a baseline rhythm changes. Try this next time you're out and about in the big city – walk down a main boulevard and set your baseline. Just stand there, people watch for a couple of minutes, and allow yourself to "feel" what that baseline rhythm feels like. Then walk away from that busy main street a considerable distance and take a seat at a quiet little café off some side street. Observe your new environment. Set your new baseline. Feel its rhythm.

Now compare the baseline rhythm you felt on the main street with that of the one you took at the café. You may notice a contrast. It is your ability to sense this contrast that may one day save your bacon should you find yourself in the middle of an active threat.

What can you do to best prepare for an active shooter at a crowded venue[41] or vehicular attack in open public, while you are on foot?

Imagine yourself walking down that same main street, setting your baseline and feeling its rhythm. You then get engrossed in a conversation with whom you are walking with, when suddenly you sense a change in the rhythm. It causes you to switch your attention from your conversation to your sensory input whereas you observe a truck increasing speed as it plows through the crowd killing and injuring people in its path and it's heading in your direction.

---

41   October 1, 2017, a gunman opened fire on a crowd of concertgoers at the Route 91 Harvest music festival on the Las Vegas Strip in Nevada, leaving 59 people dead and 547 injured

It wasn't your sensory input that provided your *earliest* possible warning. It was your detection of the change in baseline rhythm. A most valuable personal security tool should you opt to add it to your tool kit.

To increase your odds of escaping if an attack erupts, it's critical to remain cognizant of your surroundings by applying your awareness. Situation awareness must be part of your everyday carry (EDC). Stay alert for trouble and quickly recognize a threat. But, most important, you should already have mentally prepared yourself[42] to take immediate action to get out of the kill zone once you are made aware of the danger.

At the end of the day you can use your *Situational Awareness* to control your environment if you:

1. Apply your Awareness
    a. Use the four color codes to click your *personal security radar* up or down as your environment dictates, keeping a relaxed awareness for any blips on that radar.
2. Recognize a Threat
    a. Use all five senses and your sixth sense, plus your primal instincts to differentiate between *event indicators* and *threat indicators*.
    b. Spot anomalies. Use your baseline early-warning threat identification training *before* that pot of water boils over.

---

42   Think like, act like, and be a hard target!

CHAPTER 5

THREAT AVOIDANCE

"Either You Control the Threat or the Threat Controls You!"

ANONYMOUS

Either you control the threat or the threat controls you. There are no other options. To ensure your personal security is for *you* to control the threat. In traditional threat management, when bad things happen, most people believe there are only two options: either dial 911 and wait for the troops to arrive, or handle it themselves using hard skills.

Many years ago, I worked as a reserve deputy for a sheriff's office way out in the boonies of Northern Nevada. Sometimes responding to a call in such a remote area could take anywhere from thirty minutes to nearly an hour. If you called dispatch from way out there and your survival was dependent on an immediate response, then an hour late is an hour too late.

Even if you live in an incorporated city replete with nearby emergency services, time is a significant factor when managing an active threat. Two armed active shooters firing into a crowded mall and moving toward you or your family unfolds too rapidly for even emergency services who may arrive in a matter of minutes.

Should you find yourself in the middle of a violent physical threat, behind the action-reaction power curve, and you choose to handle it yourself, then you have only two options – either go to hands, that is apply a physical self-defensive technique (strike to the eyes or throat, kick to the groin, etc.) to your assailant(s) or go to guns.

If You Go to Guns You Failed

To set the record straight – *the* most effective way to stop a bad guy with a gun shooting at you, is a good guy with a gun who is trained to stop the bad guy. Anything less than that, is less than optimal. However, the opposite is also true. Just because you carry a gun doesn't mean it's your first and only line of defense regardless of the situation. In fact, it should be your very last.

The key to managing any *Active Threat* is not waiting to be caught in the middle of an attack, and then come up with a solution on the fly. It is, instead, to widen your scope of awareness prior to the attack, with the intent to predict or prevent your involvement.

The fact that you would even consider going to guns means that you've been pushed back on your heels *reacting* to the situation. Being *reactive* means you're already behind the action-reaction power curve and are forced to take immediate physical action (use your hard skills) to regain the initiative.

Back in the days when I was working in executive protection, we had a team leader (TL) who was a seasoned, salty dog. In the field for several decades and on the verge of retirement, at a pre-deployment briefing he once said to us "As protective agents, if you boys go to guns you failed."

We were dumfounded by his words as firearms training was paramount to deployment. In fact, our *hard skills* maintenance was such a high priority that if you didn't pass the firearms qualification you would not be eligible for deployment. How could he get away with saying something like that? It's because he considered firearms "lifeboats on the Titanic." His thinking was, a ship goes down due to negligence. If you go to guns as your one and only response, you have instantly raised the use of force, eliminated any other options, and placed everyone involved at higher risk.

What he was trying to make us realize was, if you rely on only one tool, the lifeboat, then you have failed miserably in your job responsibilities to protect those in your charge. Going to guns should be considered a last-ditch effort.

Aside from the reality that you're not allowed to carry a gun at the likes of airports, federal buildings, hospitals and posted businesses, consider other advantages of not going to guns.

Imagine you're in a situation that offers you two choices – go to guns (shooting solution) or don't go to guns (tactical solution). You identify an active threat and you determine that going to guns is a justifiable solution. Given your level of training, you shoot the bad guy with your gun. Further assume you succeeded in stopping the threat and, other than the bad guy, nobody else was hurt. At your criminal hearing, all was found to be by the book, your shooting was immaculate, textbook perfect, and it was determined to be completely justified.

However, the price tag in civil court for your perfectly justifiable shooting may well exceed over $150,000 in attorney's fees plus the next three to five years of your life in and out of depositions, hearings and or courtrooms. Again, that's if everything went right. What would have been the result of that same scenario if you didn't go to guns and there was another way to stop the threat? What if there was a tactical or alternate solution?

"If you go to guns you failed" means that you failed multiple opportunities to take *preventative measures* to ensure your personal security and that of those who you are responsible to protect.

Depending upon the situation, you may need a lifeboat, and if so, then yes, you certainly need to know how to use it. How about being *proactive* and using your situational awareness to look for icebergs? And if you happen to see one then how about taking *active* measures by steering the ship clear of it? What a concept – not relying on the lifeboat as your only tool.

The critical importance of choosing threat *avoidance* over threat *defense* is a game-changer when it comes to personal security.

Instead of relying on one of the two traditional responses: self-defense technique or deploying your firearm, what if there was a third option – one that doesn't require a spinning monkey back-kick to your opponent's head or going to guns?

Think of an active threat as a freight train coming straight at you and you're standing on that train's tracks. First off, *realizing* you're on the train tracks long before you even hear, see or sense a freight train, should be motivation enough for you to step off the tracks toward someplace less hazardous to your health. Taking *proactive* measures is avoiding the threat altogether before it even manifests.

Second, if you didn't realize you were standing on a set of railroad tracks, you at least had enough *situational awareness* to feel the rumble beneath your feet, hear the whistle blowing and see the red lights flashing – all very good indicators that you're about to get smashed like a bug. Observing these certain threat indicators allows you to take *active* measures in mitigating the threat, and its impact, as opposed to reacting to it.

If you fail to realize you're standing on the tracks, then you have forfeited the opportunity to take *proactive* measures. If you fail to see the oncoming threat indicators, then you have forfeited the opportunity to take *active* measures. If you didn't hear it, see it, feel it or smell it coming then you are completely taken by surprised and have no other choice but to *react* to the situation.

Illustrating your threat management options in a flow chart, it looks like:

Fig. 6 Avoid – Mitigate - Defend

The best of these three doesn't take a degree in rocket surgery. Your "A" answer is to avoid a threat altogether. If you don't stand in the middle of the railroad tracks when there's a freight train coming, then you can't possibly get hit by it. Failing avoidance, the very next best option is to use your *situational awareness* to detect threat indicators (rumbling, whistle, etc.,) and if you find any, then step away from the inbound freight train.

Going to guns is analogous to going for the lifeboats. Relying only on a shooting solution means you have found yourself at the very bottom of the avoid-mitigate-defend flowchart. It means you are not in control. You are *reacting* and attempting to regain control by shooting your way out of the situation. By going to guns you instantly direct your attacker's bullets to your position, placing yourself and those nearest you, at higher risk. Going to guns should never be your first consideration in solving any tactical problem. It should be your last.

It is important to note that not all attacks are discernable from the onset. You may just look up and see a freight train coming straight at you with absolutely no warning, and no time to do anything else but raise your eyebrows. This is known in protection parlance as a "black swan." Such events as an ambush and simply being at the wrong place at the wrong time, although very few and far between, do happen and are worth mentioning.

However, most bad things that happen to good people, are not *black swan* events and can be readily detected with minimal training.

Why did our team leader prefer *proactive measures* over *reactive measures*? Aside from the obvious reason of reducing operational risk to ourselves and our protectees, experienced had taught him that *proactive measures* establish immediate control, work any time and any place, and can give you the tactical advantage. How can you use *proactive measures* to your advantage and as a third option to defend against an active threat?

Exploit the Common Denominator

Proactive measures afford you the opportunity to look for icebergs, and even predict where to find them, long before the ship even comes close to impact. How can you know where to look for an iceberg? You start with a common denominator.

All bad things that happen to good people, whether it be a terrorist attack, an active shooting, kidnapping, mugging, or home invasion, share one thing in common. What is that common denominator, and more importantly, how can you exploit it to avoid, mitigate or even defend against an active threat?

Given the new normal, the bad news is that today's undesired events are unprecedented (never before in history could a Romanian hacker reach into your kids bedroom and watch what they were posting on their social media) and persistent (they are not going away). The good news is that we have locks, alarms, cyber-security (firewalls), cameras, security guards and first responders established as physical defenses against these undesired events. When something bad happens, it directly impacts one or more of these physical defenses.

All bad things have a start point. As they develop from bad to worse, they eventually impact these defenses scribing a *gap* between the occurrence of that event, and the physical defense set against it. It is this gap which is the common denominator shared by all undesired events.

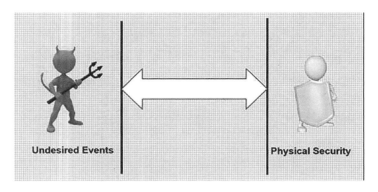

Fig 7. Common Denominator

Focusing on this gap, you can not only identify this common denominator, but you can further exploit it to provide the best possible solution to managing an *Active Threat*.

How can you exploit this common denominator? Although it's impossible to predict exactly *when* or *where* an event may occur, it is possible to know *how* an event will occur. It is this knowledge that gives you the decisive advantage over assailants or predators. Knowing how to read and effectively use the "Bad Guy's Blueprint," affords you the opportunity to avoid or control a threat.

PART II

HOW TO CONTROL A THREAT

CHAPTER 6

THE 90% ADVANTAGE

"Force has no place where there is need of skill."
HERODOTUS 425 BC

Bad Guy's Blueprint

When it comes to managing a real world physical threat, ranging from feeling uncomfortable with someone approaching you, to finding yourself in the middle of an active shooter situation or terrorist attack and everything in between, it all boils down to one question: how do you control the threat?

Step one in controlling *anything*, is knowing how that thing works. To control a moving vehicle, you need to know certain basics such as how to start and stop it, how to steer it and how to put it in gear. Without this basic knowledge, you wouldn't have the faintest clue how to control it. This same concept applies to controlling an active threat.

Recall the last time you walked in on a movie or a TV show you'd never seen before, during the last five minutes. In this short amount of time and with limited information about what you were watching, were you able to identify the characters or follow the plot? Were you aware of what had happened before you walked in, and what may be the anticipated outcome? Not possible. Unless you watched it all the way from the very beginning through to the end, there's no way to answer any of these questions.

Now recall a movie you've seen many times – something like The Godfather. You're so familiar with the plot that you can predict *exactly* what's going to happen next. Not only can you identify all the characters, plot, sub-plots, and sequence of events, but you also know; "this is the part where the guy says, 'I'll make him an offer he can't refuse.'"

You can make this claim with absolute certainty because you've seen it so many times. The same applies to the actions of any terrorist, criminal or opportunistic predator (i.e. bad guy) perpetrating an active threat.

To implement his attack, the bad guy must follow an exact formula just like a movie script. If he wants to succeed, he has no choice but to follow set steps *and* in their exact order. Your objective is to stop him, her or them, from following this script also known as the *Bad Guy's Blueprint*. Knowing how to read the *Bad Guy's Blueprint*, allows you to predict what's coming next and how to handle it.

What exactly is a *Bad Guy's Blueprint*? Taking a holistic approach to your personal security, it's important to first recognize that bad things don't happen to good people straight out of the clear blue sky. Most folks believe that suddenly, you find yourself in some dark alley in the middle of the night with your back up against the wall and a gun in your face. This is as absurd as someone who didn't notice the change in humidity and gathering of clouds before blurting out "Yeah, all of a sudden, for no reason, it just started raining!"

It all goes back to Mother Nature. Just as there is always a series of preceding events that cause inclement weather, there is always a series of preceding events that cause you to find yourself in a nasty situation. It's these series of preceding events or cycles of action, that make up the *Bad Guy's Blueprint*. Understanding how these series of preceding events, or cycles of action work, allows you to predict what's coming next – "this is the part where the guy…" You can further use that information to avoid, mitigate or defend against an active threat.

The cycle of night and day and the cycle of four seasons are examples of fundamental cycles of nature as is the cycle of birth, youth, and adulthood.

Nobody is exempt from these fundamental cycles, including the bad guys. Even Adolf Hitler started out as a helpless little baby in need of a bottle and a diaper change. We are all subject to these cycles to include natural threats, such as hurricanes and blizzards, and man-made threats such as terrorist attacks, active shootings and home invasions.

Wait a minute. How do man-made threats follow fundamental cycles? Cycles of which no bad guy is exempt? More importantly, how can your understanding of these cycles help you to avoid, mitigate or defend against an active threat? To use the *Bad Guy's Blueprint* to your advantage, you must first understand a paramount decision-making cycle that can be observed and controlled. Defense intelligence, law enforcement and protection professionals alike have discovered that controlling this interactive cycle is the key to rapid adaptation during a conflict and therefore is an essential tool to be used in defeating the bad guy's plans. This cycle is the foundation of the *Bad Guy's Blueprint*, and can be best understood by the discoveries of a recognized military strategists of the twentieth century.

OODA Loop

The cycle of how we interact with our immediate environment, was discovered by military strategist and US Air Force fighter pilot Colonel John R. Boyd (1928-1997). It is known as the *OODA Loop* and has been proven as a cornerstone in defeating threat-related behavior.

Col. Boyd served in the US Army Air Corps from 1945 to 1947 and subsequently served as an officer in the U.S. Air Force from July 1945 to August 1975.

He was known as "40-second Boyd" for his ability to best any opponent in aerial combat. From 1954 to 1960 virtually every combat pilot in the United States knew that Colonel Boyd, a former F-86 Korean War fighter pilot who helped establish the Fighter Weapons School at Nellis Air Force Base in Nevada, had a standing offer: take a position on his tail, and 40 seconds later he would have the challenger in his own gun-sights or pay $40. Back in the 1950's $40 was a lot of money and Colonel Boyd never lost the bet in more than 3,000 hours of flying time. He earned the moniker "40 Second Boyd" and was considered an icon and master level fighter pilot instructor.

When asked about the secrets to his success in aerial combat, Colonel Boyd responded with his "hypothesis" that all professionals "undergo a continuous cycle of interaction with their environment." He proposed that every human being, knowingly or unknowing uses this cycle in the process of deciding and acting.

A compressed representation of Johnson's six steps to the human processing of information, it has become known in professional circles as the *OODA Loop* and adopted by all branches of the U.S. military, civilian law enforcement, U.S. defense intelligence and professional protection communities. It is still taught at training academies to this day. Applied to your own personal security, the OODA Loop can be utilized as either a proactive measure or an active measure.

The *OODA Loop* in its most simplified form, is comprised of only four steps in the continuous cycle of interaction with our environment: *Observe, Orient, Decide,* and *Act.*

This cycle-of-action process is best described when applied to a real-world example. When you walk into a movie theater, you *observe*, where the screen is, where the stairs and the open chairs are, you *orient* to your physical position (screen in front, exit to your left, chairs behind you, etc.,) and determine the distance you are from these objects you just observed. The next step in the cycle is to *decide* in which chair you will sit. Lastly, after deciding, you *act* on that decision.

Knowingly or unknowingly we use the *OODA Loop* for everything from running a business to crossing an intersection. There is no action that we take in our daily activities that is NOT part of an *OODA Loop*. The same holds true for how bad guys operate. Working knowledge of the *OODA Loop* allows you to stay ahead of a threat by helping you make definitive and appropriate decisions quicker than your adversary.

Fig. 8. The OODA Loop

How can you use this fundamental cycle to affect a threat? Colonel Boyd developed the *OODA Loop* to describe the repeated cycle of *Observation, Orientation, Decision* and *Action* that characterized every encounter. The key to victory, he theorized, is to get inside your adversary's Loop.

In the Loop

Using the Loop as an Active Measure

We must remain interactive with our environment each time a condition changes in that environment. The condition of your environment such as inclement or fair weather, bright, low or no light, etc., the condition of your threat and the condition of yourself, can all change. A new loop begins with each change of condition, continually throughout the unfolding of an active threat.

The essential mechanics are that a fresh *OODA Loop* is run at the end of a previous cycle. In practical application of this concept, you are driving on a freeway and *observe* another vehicle occasionally swerving in and out of its lane. You *orient* to your distance, speed and position relative to the threat and *decide* to pass this vehicle. You a*ct* on your decision by applying foot pressure to the gas pedal.

However, just as you are acting on your decision and are in the acceleration process, you *observe* that same driver also accelerates, you *orient* to the situation in that he's matching your speed, so you *decide* to slow down, and a*ct* on your decision by relieving pressure on the accelerator allowing him to pass in front of you. You ran two *OODA Loops* immediately back to back with the entire incident taking place in a matter of seconds.

Reaction time plays a factor in how quickly an *OODA Loop* is run. Per former FBI Agent, senior firearms instructor, holster designer and renowned competitive shooter Bill Rogers, the average amount of time it takes for a human being to mentally react to a stimulus, or what he calls a "unit of human reaction time," is approximately .25 seconds.

Everyone's reaction time is different and the speed at which you run your loop is impacted by this factor. However, like defeating *Normalcy Bias*, just by knowing what is the *OODA Loop* and how it works, increases your familiarity with the process, which decreases your response time.

The repeated cycle is a continual stream of running through all four steps of one cycle per person per event. In other words, while you're running your *OODA Loop* the bad guy is running his. The physics of this equation is that only one of you can *act* at a time while the other *reacts* to that action. Applying this principal, you can use the *OODA Loop* as a tool to regain the initiative.

Take the Curve

Who takes control wins. The bad guy is the one who decides, when, where, and how the attack will go down. He/ they also determine what weapons will be used, and who will be their victims. Because they set these parameters, they have control of the action-reaction power curve.[43] At the onset of an attack, your objective is to take back that curve. You only need to accomplish one simple task – take back the initiative and that is, to make them react to you.

There is a very simple formula for taking the curve:

1. Bad Guy has control
2. Good guy makes bad guy react
3. Good guy takes control

---

43   In Department of Defense (DoD) parlance, they have "taken the initiative."

Following are examples of how you can use the *OODA Loop* as an active measure:

You arrive at your destination by taxi from the airport and are unloading your bags from the cab when you look up and notice two individuals posted across the street observing you handling your luggage. When they *observe* you watching them, they cease their surveillance and walk away. The entire incident took place in under a second but, what really happened was a transfer of threat control. You caused them to react and, as a result, took control.

The predators, who you couldn't initially see because you were in the taxi, were running their *OODA loop*. As criminal opportunists, they *observed* that it was a busy hotel and *oriented* to the fact that many people leave their bags unattended while their attention is focused elsewhere, *decided* that this would be a great location to position themselves and ply their nefarious craft. In acting out their decision they set up and start scanning for potential victims.

Up rolls your taxi. Your unseen adversaries immediately start their next loop and *observe* you getting out of your taxi. They then *orient* to the scenario that you're focused on talking with the driver, with your cell phone in one hand and while placing your luggage on the ground next to you. They *decide* you're a valid target and *act* on that decision by monitoring your actions while moving toward you. In following their loop to *act*, they have taken the initiative by making the first move. At this point, they have taken control of the action-reaction power curve and are currently in control of this scenario.

Stepping out of the taxi cab, you run your loop and *observe* that you're in a not-so-nice neighborhood, *orient* to the fact that you may be a potential target, so you *decide* to practice good situational awareness and *act* on that decision. By acting on your decision, you see them looking directly at you. Catching them in the act by running your *OODA Loop* you have cut inside their loop. Much like an interception in football you have reversed the play – defense has become offense. You took control of the incident by reversing possession of the action-re-action power curve. Realizing that *you* are now in control of the situation, they scurry off to look for softer targets.

Making your adversary react causes them to relinquish control. Actively using *your* OODA loop to get inside *their* loop, you force them to run a fresh loop. In doing so they must re-observe, re-orient, re-decide and (my favorite) *re-act* to the actions of your current loop. You have taken control of the action-reaction power curve the split second they react to your actions.

The terrorist, predator or opportunist carrying out any planned attack such as a home invasion, mugging, kid-napping, active shooting, etc., has no other choice but to follow the predetermined cycles of the *OODA Loop* to ensure their success. Your knowledge of the *OODA Loop*, how it works, and how you can use it as an active measure to get inside their loop enables you to retake the initiative.

Bad guy has control, you make him react, you take control – it's that easy. You're making him react, is the key to the lock. To better understand how this key works, requires drilling deeper into how the *OODA Loop* is applied to an active threat, and more importantly how you can use the *OODA Loop* proactively as part of the *Bad Guy's Blueprint* to help predict and even prevent an active threat.

Threat Progression

The *OODA Loop* is the foundation of the *Bad Guy's Blueprint* and fundamental to the development of any threat. A threat can start out being only *potential* – meaning that it has the capacity to soon develop into an active threat. The progression from *potential threat* to an active threat is best illustrated by the example of the classic schoolyard bully.

In any schoolyard, there exists a probability that there may be a bully present. If this is true, then we have accurately described a *potential threat*. Although a *potential threat*, the capable bully, standing in a schoolyard without motivation or opportunity poses no observable threat. The same bully, standing in a schoolyard running his *OODA Loop, observes* his immediate environment and thinks to himself "Easy pickings here." He then *orients* to his environment thinking to himself "Hey, I'm the biggest, baddest kid in this schoolyard and I know I can take anybody here." At this point, he remains only a *potential threat*. It's only when he moves to the next step in his *OODA Loop* that things change.

When the bully arrives at his *decision* "I'm gonna score some extra lunch money," he crosses that line of demarcation and converts from being a potential threat to an *active threat*. The *Decide* step of the *OODA Loop* is internal and not outwardly observable by anyone other than the bully until he completes his loop and *acts* on his decision. The bully, now exhibiting observable attack-related behavior, serves as a confirmation of his status as an *active threat*. Motivated by his decision and capable of carrying out his plan, the bully, completing this last step of his *OODA Loop*, exhibits *pre-attack behavior* by looking around the schoolyard for suitable prey. He then selects his victim and moves toward him, points his finger at him and raising his voice starts shouting "Hey kid, yeah you, I'm talking to you!" All this *pre-attack behavior* is observable.

The last step of his *OODA Loop*, the physical strike or *attack behavior* of the bully, ends up being a punch in the face of the victim who is subsequently relieved of his lunch money.

OODA LOOP		THREAT RELATIONSHIP
Observe	The bully takes note of his environment—the schoolyard.	Exists as a *Potential Threat*
Orient	He assesses the situation comparing himself to others.	
Decide	Based on his orientation he decides to attack.	Converts to an *Active Threat*
Act	He takes action based on his decision.	Exhibits *Pre-attack Behavior*
		Exhibits *Attack Behavior*

Fig. 9. OODA Loop – Threat Relationship

To the untrained eye, the entire incident appeared to be a single snapshot of one kid punching another kid in the face for no reason. But, to the trained observer, it is a clear illustration of the *OODA Loop* running from beginning to end of the cycle, just like the individual cells of a movie strip, describing the progression of a threat, or a *Threat Progression*.

Another example of a *Threat Progression* is a guy driving around a parking lot in a white van who *observes* an attractive female walking to her car. Whether he's trying for her phone number or something worse, he starts out as a *Potential Threat*. He then *orients* to his physical position relative to the woman and *decides* he wants more than to just look at her (becomes an *Active Threat*). He *acts* on that decision by driving toward her (exhibiting *Pre-Attack Behavior*) and pulling up directly next to her within an arm's reach and engaging her verbally or physically (exhibiting *Attack Behavior*).

Using the classic mugging model, you find yourself at the ATM in the middle of the night. A bad, *Potential Threat*, *observes* you walking from your car alone, lost in conversation on your cell, and oblivious to your surroundings. He *orients* to your lack of situational awareness, physical position relative to the ATM and your car. Upon *deciding* to target you as his next victim, he converts to an *Active Threat*. He *acts* on that decision and moves in toward you (exhibiting *Pre-Attack Behavior*) and engages you in conversation or at gunpoint (exhibiting *Attack Behavior*).

Fig. 10. Threat Progression

A *Threat Progression* makes up the middle layer of the *Bad Guy's Blueprint* and like the OODA Loop, can be used as a tool to help you avoid, mitigate or defend against an active threat.

Attack-Related Behavior

Since it's not possible to read someone's mind, their true intentions can't be discovered until they take physical action. Although there's not much you can do to affect the first fifty percent of a *Threat Progression* (conversion of a potential threat to an active threat), there's plenty you can do to avoid, mitigate or defend against the threat when you can identify and manage both pre-attack and attack behavior which are collectively referred to as *attack-related behavior*.

Fig. 11. Attack-Related Behavior

Using your situational awareness, you can readily observe the last fifty percent of a *Threat Progression* or attack-related behavior. To manage this behavior, like using the *OODA Loop* as an active measure, requires a deeper understanding of these behaviors and how they work. All predators—human or animal that have moved from a *potential threat* to an *active threat*, and are about to move into *attack-related behavior*, share one thing in common: they *must* complete yet another fundamental cycle of action to be successful. The steps of this cycle of action are what define *attack-related behavior* and are best illustrated by travelling with your mind's eye to the Serengeti[44].

The Attack Cycle

In the Serengeti, the lion is motivated by hunger. Upon his decision to hunt, converts from a *potential threat* to an *active threat*. He commences his attack-related behavior by *looking* for a tasty impala. Step 1 – Look.

There are two impalas – one with his head buried in the deep grass intently grazing, unaware of his predicament, and the other impala with its head up, eyes and ears trained in the direction of the lion's gaze. The lion must then choose his prey. Step 2 – Choose. From the lion's point of view, which of these critters has a less than optimal future? Of course, the oblivious one. Why? Because he is completely tuned out from his environment.

---

44   The Serengeti ecosystem is a geographical region in Africa located in northern Tanzania and into south-western Kenya

The next step in the natural process is to stalk. Step 3 – Stalk. When stalking, the lion does two things: A. Verify: Focus on his prey (closely observe) and confirms that prey is indeed his best target. In protective intelligence parlance, this is "confirming target selection" and is accomplished by verifying that this target is truly the best choice. If the lion observes that his potential prey, is alerted to the pending attack, then he's probably not the best choice. B. Plan: Upon verification, the predator plans how to close in on his prey.

Completing the stalk phase, target verification and planning, it's now time to execute the plan by moving from his current physical position to one of tactical advantage in preparation for attack. Step 4 – Close in.

Finally, in position, the final step in the cycle is to execute the attack. Step 5 – Attack.

Fig. 12. The Attack Cycle

Known as the *Attack Cycle*, each step of this fundamental cycle represents the individual movie frames of *Attack Related Behavior* within a *Threat Progression* from *pre-attack behavior* to *attack behavior*. In the animal kingdom, the *Attack Cycle* ensures the balance of the ecosystem. In the human kingdom, the *Attack Cycle* directly applies to human predators. In the case of a human predator, the bad guy also must first seek his prey. He will not target you if you don't give him a reason to find interest in you. In the process of seeking, he must look for and choose his target. These two steps, *Look* and *Choose*, MUST occur in order.

Following the *Look* and *Choose* steps, the human predator must then *Stalk* his prey. He may observe you for a while, figure out if you're worth the effort; maybe you are, maybe you're not. Once he makes his decision he then needs to figure out how to close in on you. Again, these are mandatory steps, *Look*, *Choose*, and *Stalk*, that must be executed in order. If he decides that you're not worth the effort, then he's not going to move to the next step in his plan - *Close*.

After *looking*, *choosing*, and *stalking* he is then tasked with *closing* the gap from his physical position, to your physical position. Lastly and only after these first four steps, *Look*, *Choose*, *Stalk* and *Close*, will he be in the right place and at the right time to execute his planned attack.

The *Attack Cycle*, in the defense intelligence community, represents the execution of these five steps in order, which any predator must follow to present you with a physical threat. An integral part of the *Bad Guy's Blueprint*, he must follow all five steps. He cannot omit even one and cannot execute them out of order. They must be followed one at a time and in this exact sequence or, he fails.

Now that you're familiar with this third component of the *Bad Guy's Blueprint* and how it works, you can use this knowledge to disrupt his plan. All you need to do is burn him, make him react one time, at any step of the *Attack Cycle*, and his plans are compromised. Disrupt his plan and you take control of the threat.

The *Bad Guy's Blueprint* is comprised of three integrated parts: Foundationally, the *OODA Loop* describes the continuous cycle of decisive human interaction with our environment. The next layer, a *Threat Progression*, represents the threat status of that continuous cycle. The third piece of the *Bad Guy's Blueprint* is the *Attack Cycle*, which illustrates the individual steps of attack-related behavior. Knowing what is, and how to read the *Bad Guy's Blueprint*, provides you with a predetermined script – one the bad guys MUST follow to the letter, to be successful.

OODA Loop	Observe	Orient	Decide	Act				
Threat Progression	Potential Threat		Active Threat	Pre-attack Behavior		Attack Behavior		
Attack Cycle				Look	Choose	Stalk	Close	Attack

Figure 13. The Bad Guy's Blueprint

The *Bad Guy's Blueprint* can be used to gain the upper hand in the event of an active threat. Each layer can be used as an individual problem-solving tool. You can use your *OODA Loop* either actively or proactively. Actively, to get inside your opponent's loop forcing him to react, allowing you to retake the the action-reaction power curve. Proactively, to identify a threat status.

Understanding a *Threat Progression* allows you to assess the real-time status, and identify the attack-related behaviors of a developing threat. Knowing how the *Attack Cycle* works gives you the ability to identify each of the steps to a successful attack, and as such, the opportunity to break any of them along the way to stop the attack.

Using the *Bad Guy's Blueprint* can certainly be beneficial in monitoring the status of an active threat, but how can it be used more effectively to *prevent* or *avoid* an active threat altogether? Although it may not tell you *when* or *where* an undesired event may occur, the *Bad Guy's Blueprint* can tell *how* it will occur, allowing you to predict what's coming next in the unfolding of an active theat. And in doing so, the opportunity to prevent it.

CHAPTER 7

PREDICTABLE IS PREVENTABLE

"If it's predictable, it's preventable."
GORDON GRAHAM

A *Threat Progression* is a predictable timeline of foreseeable events. As such, "if it's predictable it's preventable.[45]" Since September 11th, 2001 there have been dozens of documented cases where federal agencies were able to uncover and foil terrorist attempts using the *Bad Guy's Blueprint* to disrupt their plans and prevent the threat

---

45   Keynote speaker and retired California Highway Patrol Officer Gordon Graham, referencing an active threat

from occurring.[46] Some of these you see in the news.[47] However, most you don't, as the agencies are careful to not divulge their methods and practices, and rightfully so. What tools can you take and keep in your kit that can be gleaned from nearly two decades of counterterrorism efforts? Knowing how to interpret a threat progression timeline.

Threat Progression Timeline

Your significant other, one of your kids, or grandkids, is walking across the parking lot and is suddenly approached by a stranger asking for money. The entire incident occurred in a matter of seconds. A professional hacker working from a foreign country trying to break into your social media may take a few days. Kidnappers planning an abduction might take a couple of weeks and a burglar could case out a neighborhood for as long as a month or more.

Regardless of how much time it takes for each of these undesired events to unfold, once activity moves past step three of the *Attack Cycle*, the time line is exponentially accelerated when crossing the line into Step 4 and propelling into Step 5.

Much like determining where a car or an airplane will be located at a future time and place based on current position and speed, determining the progression of an

---

46   https://thf_media.s3.amazonaws.com/2013/pdf/SR137.pdf- Page 8 of the report (see chart).

47   http://www.detroitnews.com/story/news/local/wayne-county/2016/02/05/feds-dearborn-hts-man-supports-isis-planned-attack/79906302/

active threat on a timeline makes its position and speed the most predictable elements.

Fig. 14. All attacks accelerate at steps 4 and 5

Focusing on these discernable elements (position and speed), the entire *Bad Guy's Blueprint* can be compressed into a single predictable timeline with a measurable position (between steps 4 and 5) and speed (maximum acceleration) referred to in the US DoD community as "bang".

Back in the1990's and later when I was working as a contractor for the United States Government (USG) including US DoD, I had heard the term "bang" used throughout the community and was familiar with the concepts of its avoidance and prevention. However, it wasn't until Patrick Van Horne and Jason A. Riley published their book "Left of Bang – How The Marine Corps' Combat Hunter Program

Can Save Your Life,"[48] that *bang* was effectively introduced outside the DoD community. If you haven't read this one yet, you need it in your library!

Many of my students, a majority in the protection field, have read "Left of Bang" and ask me how it integrates with a *Threat Progression* and how they can leverage that intersect to increase their effectiveness in the field. Having answered the question so many times in person, I thought it best to include it here starting with *what* is *bang*.

What is Bang?

When there's an explosion, things around that explosion blow up. Violence is an explosion of aggressive force. If you are involved in that explosion you can and will get hurt. Zeroing in on this exact point, authors Van Horne and Riley define *bang*:

"If you were to think of an attack on a timeline, bang is in the middle. Bang is the act. Bang is the IED [Improvised Explosive Device] explosion, the sniper taking the shot, or the beginning of an ambush. Bang is what we want to prevent. Being left of bang means that a person has observed the pre-event indicators, one of the warning signs, that must occur earlier on the timeline for the bang to happen."[49]

Speaking as a protective agent, and coming from the personal security perspective, *bang* is the impact with

---

48   https://www.amazon.com/Left-Bang-Marine-Combat-Program/
      dp/1936891301 Published in June 2014
49   Left of Bang – How the Marine Corps' Combat Hunter Program Can Save
      Your Life" Page 15-16

that iceberg you're trying to avoid. It's the undesired event that affects you and those around you. *Bang* can range from a natural disaster like a hurricane (Katrina), which takes days or even weeks to approach, or a manmade event (London Bridge) on or near you by one or more persons using all manner of nastiness to include bombs, guns, trucks, hazardous materials, non-ballistic weapons and the like. *Bang* is the deadliest part of an active threat.

Staying "left of bang" requires that you first are aware that there is such a thing as *bang*. As covered earlier, part of being a hard target means that you also need to be aware that *bang* can happen to you not in some far-off distant imagined scenario. It could happen the next time you walk into a movie theater, night club, doctor's office, outdoor music concert, restaurant, airport or in the very next moment when you walk out that door. In the new normal, we are all subject to *bang* – no one is exempt.

Where is Bang?

In concurrence with Van Horne and Riley referencing the timeline of an undesired event, bang occurs somewhere "in the middle" of that timeline. To leverage an intersect from the protective services perspective, I want to focus on precisely *where* in the middle of that timeline it occurs, and *why* this is so critically important.

Where exactly is *bang*? Referencing the *Bad Guy's Blueprint*, *bang* is located at a measurable position along a predictable timeline (*Threat Progression*).

It is the precise instance of maximum acceleration (explosion) on that line of demarcation between steps 4 (close) and 5 (attack) – at the very onset of the physical attack.

Threat Progression	Potential Threat	Active Threat	Pre-attack Behavior		Attack Behavior		
Attack Cycle			Look	Choose	Stalk	Close	Attack

Fig. 15 Where bang occurs on the timeline

Why is this so important? As was covered earlier, it is your attacker(s) who determine(s), when, where and how it will go down, who will be hit and with what method, personnel and equipment. Those decisions are what give them the initiative (control of the action-reaction power curve) - a considerable tactical advantage right out the gate. From the predator's optic, *Bang* is the most effective control point of a *Threat Progression*.

To "*the right of bang*"[50] you are relegated to reaction. Things have gotten physically violent, and demand physical response. Here, on the timeline, you are one hundred percent reliant on your *hard* skills, potentially raising your *Scale of Injury*, and significantly reducing your tactical options. You are behind the curve and have lost the initiative. Until you take control of that curve and regain the initiative, you will continue to react – out of control.

It is exponentially more difficult *right of bang*, if not impossible in some cases, to regain the initiative, (retake the action-reaction power curve) and take control of the threat. It is this exact reason why staying *left of bang* is so critical.

---

50   Van Horne and Riley

Bang is impact with the iceberg. You want to stay clear of the iceberg. Using the *Bad Guy's Blueprint* to steer clear of it is your very best bet. How can you use the *Bad Guy's Blueprint* to steer clear of an iceberg?

CHAPTER 8

AVOID, MITIGATE, DEFEND

> "There is a difference between interest and commitment. When you are interested in something, you do it when it is convenient. When you are committed, you accept no excuses...only results."
>
> **KENNETH BLANCHARD**

The *Bad Guy's Blueprint*, like any other blueprint, is used by the professionals to produce the best possible results. The four phases of a *Threat Progression* each represent twenty five percent of the entire threat development process. The last fifty percent of the attack-related behaviors can be further divided into five, ten-percent blocks representing each step of the *Attack Cycle*. The very last block, only ten percent of a *Threat Progression*, describes the actual attack itself.

25%	25%	25%		25%		
Potential Threat	Active Threat	Pre-attack Behavior		Attack Behavior		
50%		50%				
		Look	Choose	Stalk	Close	Attack
		10%	10%	10%	10%	10%
90%						10%
Soft Skills						Hard Skills

Fig. 16. Anatomy of the Bad Guy's Blueprint

Hard skills are not applicable left of bang and soft skills don't work right of bang. Hard skills exist solely for the ten percent and soft skills for the ninety percent.

Your worry and concerned is about the dreaded ten percent – requiring mastery of hard skills (using a gun, going hands-on, etc.,) but what about using the ninety percent? What about all that wide-open space and opportunity from the very beginning of a *Threat Progression* all the way through and including the very last moment left of bang – the *Close* step of the *Attack Cycle*?

The *Bad Guy's Blueprint* demonstrates that 90% of personal security is soft skills. It's what our team leader was talking about years ago when he said; "If you go to guns you failed." He meant that you failed to use the 90%.

How can you take full advantage of the opportunity to solve a personal security problem *before* needing to rely on your hard skills? The answer is to gain the decisive advantage over your assailant(s) by taking control of that first 90% of a *Threat Progression*, what I call *the 90% Advantage*.

Exploiting the Timeline

The 90% Advantage is divided into two distinctive courses of action referencing an active threat – avoidance (proactive measures) and mitigation (active measures). Failing the 90% Advantage, your only remaining option is to defend against the threat (reactive measures). As covered earlier, these are your only threat management options.

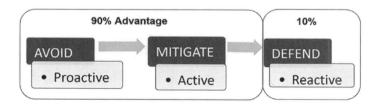

Fig. 17. Exploiting the Threat Progression Timeline

Avoidance is nothing more than stepping off those railroad tracks and not putting yourself in front of that freight train in the first place. It is a proactive measure. Measured from the very onset of a *Threat Progression*, all the way through and including the middle step 3 (stalk) of the *Attack Cycle* (between verify and plan), *the 90% Advantage* affords you unlimited options in the maximum amount of time, with the maximum opportunity and the least amount of physical risk to solve the problem. It is this wide-open space along the timeline where you may apply *proactive measures.*

Mitigation is what you do to limit the cascading of negative effects of an undesired event already in motion. It is an active measure. Measured from the middle of step 3 on the way to the very edge of bang (start of the last ten percent), affords you limited options, less time, and the need for more effort. It is this diminished battlespace along the timeline, where you may apply *active measures.*

Defense is when you can no longer avoid or mitigate the threat. It begins when your soft skills are no longer applicable. It is a reactive measure.

Measured from the very onset of the last ten percent (bang), you no longer have the luxury of using your soft skills. You have no other choice but to rely on your hard skills as things have gone physical. You have only three remaining options (covered later), the least amount of time and maximum amount of effort as things have gone physical. It is in this very narrow margin of space along the timeline – usually a matter of seconds, where you may apply your *reactive measures.*

Potential Threat	Active Threat	Step 1 Look	Step 2 Choose	VERIFY	Step 3 Stalk	PLAN	Step 4 Close	Step 5 Attack

The 90% Advantage			BANG 10%
Soft Skills			Hard Skills
Avoid		Mitigate	Defend
Unlimited Options		Limited Options	3 Options
Maximum Amount of Time		Less Time	Least Time
Least Amount of Effort		More Effort	Max Effort

Fig. 18. Anatomy of the 90% Advantage

The 90% Advantage is about taking control. You can take control by using either *proactive measures* or *active measures*.

Proactive Measures

Given the Merriam Webster definition of proactive[51], with *Proactive Measures* you can use your soft skills to take control of the biggest chunk of any *Threat Progression*.

Definition of *Proactive*: "Creating or controlling a situation by causing something to happen rather than responding to it after it has happened."

Notice the first three words, controlling a situation. As an example, Mr. Smith was attending a weekend neighborhood BBQ where he heard that there had been a rash of break-ins in his very same city block. After leaving the party, Smith decided that he was not going to be

---

51   http://www.merriam-webster.com/dictionary/proactive

the next home invasion target in the neighborhood. He went home, stocked up on ammo, installed more exterior motion-sensor lights and decreased the food for his Dobermans. Odds are stacked in his favor that any home invader would bypass his home and select another target.

Proactive measures are about not putting yourself on the railroad tracks in the first place. There's no need to go to the ATM at 2AM in a bad neighborhood. There is no need to travel to a war zone for your summer vacation.

Proactive measures are about not being attractive to the predator. Parking at a gas station convenience store, or walking into the store leaving your car door open with the engine running makes you attractive. Walking around with cash hanging out of your purse or pocket or being belligerent or drunk in public are what make you attractive.

Being proactive is about making a predator ask the question "Are there softer targets?" and the answer "Yes" *before* selecting you as prey.

Proactive measures can be applied to you personally, how you dress, where you go, your home, your car, your office, your business, and your family.

Active Measures

Given the Merriam Webster definition of *active*[52], with *Active Measures* you can use your soft skills to take control of the next biggest chunk of any *Threat Progression*.

---

52   http://www.merriam-webster.com/dictionary/active

Definition of *Active*: "Causing activity or change characterized by action rather than by contemplation." In plain speak, this means doing something as opposed to thinking about it.

Because he had to work that weekend, Mr. Wesson missed the neighborhood BBQ, but did notice a stranger snooping around the street outside the gate in front of his home in the middle of the day when he came home for lunch on the following Monday. Wesson cordially engaging the stranger in light conversation, smiled all the while and asked him non-aggressively and neighborly questions about the nice weather, if he needed any directions and the like, which shooed him away. Mr. Wesson additionally snapped out his cell phone and recorded the stranger and his license plate as he drove away. Odds are stacked greatly in Wesson's favor that if this stranger was casing the neighborhood, he won't be coming back anytime soon.

Active measures are about observing threat indicators, having the will and making the decision, to act against that indicator in a timely manner. Active measures are about doing something to turn the heat down or off that pot of hot water.

Active measures are about making a predator ask the question "Are there softer targets?" and the answer, "Yes" when he's right smack in the middle of his *Attack Cycle*.

Proactive and active measures are about taking control. Taking control means you are taking responsibility for your own personal security and taking action in the early stages of a *Threat Progression*. Proactive and active measures afford you optimal control of an active threat left of bang.

Reactive Measures

Using the Merriam Webster definition of *reactive*[53], defines when you can no longer use your soft skills and are relegated to only use of your hard skills to regain control of the last ten percent of a *Threat Progression*.

Definition of *Reactive*: "Acting in response to a situation rather than creating or controlling it."

There was a third neighbor living on that same city block, a Mr. Jones. Jones attended the BBQ and although aware of the home invasion warnings, thought to himself, "Yeah, it'll never happen to me and my family." He even watched his next-door neighbor Mr. Wesson approach the stranger lurking in front of their homes, and thought "Look, see, someone else will handle it!"

Later that night Jones was rudely awoken from a deep sleep by the sound of crashing glass from his kitchen window. Bang! He sat up in his bed wide-eyed and panic-stricken, because it was at that very moment that he realized he had lost all opportunity to control the threat. Now the threat controlled him. No longer able to use proactive or active measures, Jones was forced into only one remaining option and that was *reactive measures* in defense against the threat.

---

53   http://www.merriam-webster.com/dictionary/reactive

Reactive measures are nothing but pure hard skills. It means you're not in control and need to take back control by either taking flight and running from the threat, or using your hands/ guns and fight, to solve the tactical problem. The purpose of reactive measures is to make your attacker(s) react. Unlike Smith and Wesson, who took control of the threat using their soft skills, Jones was left with only one remaining choice – to act in response to the situation rather than creating or controlling it, using hard skills.

Unless you are a first responder where it's your job to move toward flying bullets and burning buildings, being reactive is the worst-case scenario because your response options are greatly diminished. These remaining response options are are only three – flight, fight or freeze, which will be covered in more detail later.

Reactive measures are about making a predator react and ask himself the question "Are there softer targets?" and the answer, "Yes" in the heat of Step 5 of the *Attack Cycle* - to the right of bang.

If forced to use reactive measures, you want to be that nasty, ornery, sharp, pointy, annoying critter that the bear tries put in his mouth and devour, but gives up out of shear frustration, drops his interest in you, and looks for something soft and chewy instead.

Time Space Relationship

The longer you wait on the timeline the less *time, options and opportunity* you have and the more effort it takes to solve the problem. Conversely, more time buys you more options and opportunity. *The 90% Advantage* affords you *Proactive Measures* and *Active Measures*, all long the timeline ending with *Reactive Measures* at the last ten percent.

How can the *90% Advantage* and the *Bad Guy's Blueprint* be used to avoid, mitigate or defend against a threat? You are afforded unlimited options and the maximum amount of time to solve the problem using soft skills left of bang. Bad things just don't pop in out of the blue. It is critical that you understand the *Bad Guy's Blueprint*. Just like the movies, knowing that "this is the part where the bad guy..." affords you the control to disrupt those plans using your soft skills by breaking the cycle at the earlier steps.

Knowing this, why would you ever wait for the last 10% of a *Threat Progression* where you have the least amount of options, the least amount of time and are forced to rely solely upon your hard skills to solve the tactical problem? Exploiting the one common denominator shared by all undesired events, *The 90% Advantage* gives you control of a *Threat Progression* by introducing *avoidance* and *mitigation* using proactive and active measures as opposed to relying solely on your limited hard skills for defense.

Using The *90% Advantage* to control the threat, before the threat controls you, puts you at the helm and allows you to spot an iceberg and, if need be, navigate around it.

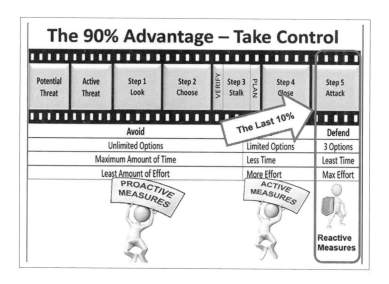

Fig. 19. The 90% Advantage

PART III

HOW TO DEFEAT
AN ATTACK

CHAPTER 9

THE ANATOMY OF AN ATTACK

> ## "Invincibility lays in the defense; the possibility of victory in the attack."
> ### SUN TZU

The fight starts before the fight starts, so to know how to defeat an attack you must first understand the anatomy of an attack. How an attack works is much like what is needed to start a fire. If you wanted to start a fire, you'd need three things: a heat source, oxygen and fuel. Put all three of them together and you could start a fire. Take away any one of these three items and it's not possible to start a fire. The same applies to executing a successful attack. If the bad guy wants to execute a successful attack then he needs three required items:

1.   A Target (potential victim)
2.   A Bad Guy (at least one bad guy - himself)
3.   A Process (to carry out the attack)

Analogous to the above fire starter example, take away any one of these three elements it wouldn't be possible for the bad guy to execute a successful attack.

The bad guy has no other options and needs all three elements. He needs a target. If you don't show up for a mugging, then you can't get mugged![54] If you deny him his opportunity, then he cannot execute his plans. If you cause him to react, then he has lost control and cannot achieve success. Remove any one element and you stop the attack. How can you do this? By affecting any of the elements using *the 90% Advantage*.

You can affect the target (you), you can affect the bad guy (your attacker(s)), and you can affect the process (Step 5 of the *Attack Cycle*) – any of which will help you avoid, mitigate or defend against an active threat. You can affect both the target and the bad guy *left of bang* using your soft skills (proactive and active measures). To the *right of bang*, you can affect the attack process (at step five), using your hard skills (reactive measures).

Affect the Target

How can you affect the target – that is you! At the very beginning of the *Attack Cycle* the predator has no other option but to follow step one and *look* for a suitable

---

54   Quote from retired USMC Intel Officer Patrick Henry

target. Completing Step 1 (Look), he must then *choose* his target (Step 2) and then verify that he has made the best target selection (verify - first half of Step 3). How can you break the *Attack Cycle* early on, between step 1 and the middle of step three? By using *Proactive Measures*.

Avoid the iceberg altogether. "Don't go to stupid places. Don't hang out with stupid people. Don't do stupid things.[55]"

At the earliest stages of the *Attack Cycle*, the odds of you stopping the attack are stacked in your favor. Here's what you've got going for you: Throughout the first half of the *Attack Cycle* you are in condition yellow (public mode). You are alert and attuned to your environment. You have unlimited options, a maximum amount of time with the least amount of effort to execute your *Proactive Measures*.

To the predator, if you capture his interest, then he/ they will target you. In simpler terms, if you look like food you will be eaten[56]. Using *Proactive Measures*, you are afforded both the time and opportunity to affect the target by not appearing like food. It's simply a matter of eliminating *Soft Target (you) Indicators*.

The Predator's Optic

What are *Soft Target Indicators*? Just like threat indicators clue you in that there could be a potential threat, *Soft Target Indicators* clue the predator in that you could be a potential target (victim or prey).

---

55   Quote from John S. Farnam, deputy sheriff, decorated Vietnam War veteran and respected defensive firearms instructor.

56   Quote from Clint Smith

In a classic study conducted by a prison psychologist where dozens of convicted felons were interviewed, the psychologist played videos or presented photos of random crowds of people in shopping malls, subway stations, and busy city streets and asked each of the inmates to point out the softest target in each photo or video—that is the individual that they would most likely attack if given the opportunity. All responses were recorded. The study concluded that nearly every inmate selected the same people in each segment for similar reasons—these reasons form the baseline definition of *Soft Target Indicators.*

Examples that help describe a *Soft Target Indicator* come from snippets of those recorded study responses, and include "looks sheepish," "eyes were looking down," "obviously lost," "an easy mark," "looks out of place," "not paying attention," "distracted," and the most common—"unaware of their surroundings." *Soft Target Indicators* can be anything along these lines that a predator might outwardly observe about you from his optic that sends him a clear message that you are easy prey.

As every case is unique according to its own specific set of circumstances, there are no hard and fast rules to unequivocally define a *Soft Target Indicator* other than any appearance or activity that screams out "Hey look over here, I'm an easy target, pick me!" to a predator. Similarly, your car, your home and even your online presence, may exhibit *Soft Target Indicators* to the opportunity-seeking predator. In most cases two or three solid *Soft Target Indicator* are enough to capture the attention of a predator.

In a more recent psychological profiling study, participants were 47 male prisoners in a Canadian maximum-security facility, many with multiple offenses. Researchers used the prisoners' scores on Robert Hare's scale of psychopathy — the Psychopathy Check List (PCL). Special attention was paid to the part of the PCL score (Factor 1) associated with interpersonal traits such as manipulativeness, superficial charm, and lack of empathy which can facilitate the exploitation of others.

The prisoners watched 12 videos. They rated each target's vulnerability to being victimized on a 10-point rating scale. Victimization was defined as "assault with the intent to rob or steal from the victim." Prisoners told how they identified those most vulnerable to being robbed. The answers were coded and distilled into categories. The cues used by prisoners were: gait, body posture (body movements not related to gait), age, gender, attractiveness, build, clothing, attention, fitness, environment (e.g., lack of lighting), and whether target was alone.

The top cues to vulnerability were: Walk/gait – walking with confidence versus walking like a *soft target*. Gender - females appear as softer targets than males. Body type - In good physical shape (could put up more of a fight) versus heavy set or slow (less physically challenging). Fitness level - Greater probability of fighting back versus unable to defend self. Attention to surroundings versus Not paying attention; Appears to be cautious versus appears to be clueless.

In distilling the above, there are three overarching *Soft Target Indicators* that command a predator's attention at first glance. These are; if you appear to be:

1. *Weak* - physically, mentally or otherwise
2. *Unaware* - distracted (lack of situational awareness) clearly not paying attention to your immediate surroundings - including them watching you
3. *Alone* - easily accessible, vulnerable, exposed, or some combination thereof

It's okay to appear weak or unaware or alone, you can appear to be any one of these, or even two of these, but if you appear to be all three: weak, unaware and alone, then you look like food! To a predator finding someone who appears weak, unaware and alone is like hitting 777 on a slot machine in Las Vegas – he just hit the proverbial jackpot.

Fig. 20. Soft target Indicators

A predator may look at many potential targets and in doing so may find two or three equally suitable candidates. As he further studies what may appear to be equally qualified targets, he makes his final decision based on their *Soft Target Indicators*.

In terms of structural targets such as homes, schools, businesses and the like, *Soft Target Indicators* may include open doors, unlocked gates, unmanned desks, etc. However, the predator changes his perspective when the building has clearly visible locks, alarms, cameras and the most effective deterrent of all – a human being with eyes on him – able to identify him for authorities. These are all indicators to the bad guy that there are softer targets.

Bad guys tend to shy away from hard targets and are drawn to *softer targets*, as they are much easier to victimize.[57] Another *Soft Target Indicator* a predator looks for to identify prey, is a breach in information security.

Information Security

We as a nation have become desensitized to information sharing – a condition which renders us prone to compromising informational security.

Predators start the *Attack Cycle* by immediately scanning the vicinity looking for soft targets. They constantly look

---

57   United States Department of Homeland Security US National Strategy for the Physical Protection of Critical Infrastructures and Key Assets quote "*[they] are relentless and patient...[they] are also opportunistic and flexible. They learn from experience and modify their tactics and targets to exploit perceived vulnerabilities and avoid observed strengths. As [protection] increases around more predictable targets, they shift their focus to less protected [targets]*"

for *Soft Target Indicators*, listen for opportunities and evaluate whether you appear to be a soft or hard target. You don't want to yell over your neighbor's fence, "Hey Joe, we're going on vacation for the next two weeks and there won't be anyone here at all for the entire time, would you pick up our mail?"

Burglars use online real-estate virtual tours to do their casing. Predators also scan the internet for low hanging social media fruit. A classic example of a post on Facebook replete with photos is, "We're so excited about our brand new in-home theater oversized flat-screen TV plus state of the art audio, but we're going to have to leave it for an entire month as we'll be vacationing in Mexico starting tomorrow!!!!"

You have control of all your outgoing information. Use that control with discretion, as there are bad guys out there who's full-time occupation is to use it against you and your family.

Keeping Information Security or INFOSEC[58] accounts for only one of many *proactive measures* you can use to remove yourself as a target from the anatomy of an attack. Bottom line about affecting the target (you) by eliminating your *Soft Target Indicators*, is to remain unattractive to the predator. Be like the gray man and blend into the environment. Be like the protective agent who, practicing good situational awareness, remains a hard target causing the predator to ask the question, "Are there softer targets?" and the answer, "Yes."

---

58   Information Security is known as INFOSEC in defense intelligence parlance.

Regardless if you choose to accept it or not, predators observe you and decide if they are interested in you. If you do everything in your control to avert that interest, you're off to a great start!

You may very well have disrupted the *Anatomy of an Attack* by eliminating any *Soft Target Indicators* before even leaving your home, at which point the *Attack Cycle* will cease to exist for you. When that solution works, you will most likely never notice its success.

Eliminating *Soft Target Indicators* is nothing more than taking proactive measures to ensure your personal security. It's about avoiding the threat altogether. It's your "A" answer to the oncoming freight train – don't step onto those train tracks in the first place!

Specific Proactive Measures

What are *specific* proactive measures to protect you from being a target? To eliminate your *Soft Target Indicators* and practice good INFOSEC is a solid foundation. However, the answer is not to just follow a few tips. Yes, these can help, but the totality of your personal security must be viewed from a holistic perspective.

As there are countless scenarios and circumstances surrounding any potential or active threat, there are equally as many countermeasures. It is unrealistic to ask for "quick tips" or "specific" *proactive measures* for every current or emerging threat, as all active threats unfold under completely different conditions. Nonetheless, there are certain established guidelines for protection professionals that you can follow to gain similar benefit. Although helpful, these are not tips such as, "Roll up your car windows and lock your doors." The practical answer, like living an active lifestyle, is living the *personal security lifestyle.*

If you want to lose weight then, motivated by your personal commitment, you must be conscious of your diet (food intake), exercise (burning calories) as both affect your weight. If you are a devout religious person, motivated by your beliefs, you strictly adhere to the tenets of your faith. Similarly, a trained protection professional such as a protective agent, or a clandestine services officer (gray man), realize they operate in the new normal, understand how to defeat normalcy bias, and realize the importance of training and how it builds their skills and confidence. Each adopts the personal security mindset, maintains mental toughness and strives to be hard targets by living a *personal security lifestyle* (applying their situational awareness to control their environment and knowing how to defeat an attack).

Neither will knowingly place themselves in a precarious situation. Each knows to blend in and remain unattractive by not exhibiting any *Soft Target Indicators*, (to include drunk in public, belligerent, etc.) Both the protective agent and the gray man alike, by living a personal security lifestyle, make any potential adversary ask the question "Are there softer targets?" and provide the answer, "Yes."

If you choose to live a healthy lifestyle, you don't just don't stop eating donuts and park further from the office door. Yes, these tips can help you of course, but the totality of a healthy lifestyle is making the commitment to be healthy by adopting the healthy lifestyle mindset and accepting the responsibility that your health is your responsibility. You practice good eating habits, follow a specific diet, exercise regimen and get regular check-ups. Maybe you take supplements or vitamins or even hire a nutritionist to help you reach your goal(s) and optimal health profile. The same applies to living a personal security lifestyle. The totality of living a personal security lifestyle is making the commitment to your own security and that of your family by adopting the mindset, accepting the responsibility and everyday practice of good situational awareness. Such repetitive practice can physically change your brain.

Change Your Brain

Dr. Lara Boyd, Brain Researcher and Professor at the University of British Columbia, received over 14 million hits in her December 2015 TEDx talk in which she addresses how we learn[59].

Dr. Boyd provides insightful perspective of our understanding human physiology as it relates to behavior. She explains why and how behavior changes your brain. The more you practice, the more you change your brain to retain long term learning.

> "In the last quarter century there has been tremendous discoveries about the functionality of the human brain. The most interesting and transformative of these discoveries is that every time you learn a new fact or skill, you change your brain. In the field of neuroscience, this is

---

59   https://www.youtube.com/watch?v=LNHBMFCzznE

called *neuroplasticity*. Research demonstrates that behavior changes your brain. These changes are not limited by age and happen all the time. The key to these changes is neuroplasticity. What does this look like?

Your brain can change in three basic ways to support learning; chemically, structurally and functionally. The first of these is chemical. Your brain functions by transferring chemical signals between brain cells (neurons) and this triggers a series of actions and reactions. To support learning your brain can increase the amount or the concentration of these chemical signaling taking place between neurons. Because this change can happen rapidly, this supports short-term learning.

The second way that the brain can change to support learning is by altering its structure. During learning the brain can change the connections between neurons. Here the physical structure of the brain is changing, and this takes time. These types of changes are related to long term memory or skills improvement. These processes interact."

To demonstrate this interaction, Dr. Boyd provides the example of trying to learn a new motor skill, learning the piano or how to juggle. She goes on to explain that you've had the experience of getting better within a single session of practice and thinking "I've got it!" and then maybe you return the next day and all those improvements from the day before are lost. What happened?

As Dr. Boyd states, "In the short term, your brain could increase the chemical signaling between your neurons. However, for some reason, those changes did not induce the structural changes necessary to support long term learning. Long term memory takes time. What you see in the short term doesn't support learning, but familiarization. It's the physical changes of the brain that support long term memory and the chemical changes that support short term memory."

Structural changes can also lead to integrated networks of brain regions that function together to support learning. They can also lead to certain brain regions that are important for very specific behaviors to change your structure or to enlarge. Dr. Lara goes on to provide examples of this. One such example is people who read braille have larger hand sensory areas in the brain than those of us who do not, dominant hand regions in the brain are larger than the non-dominant side, and how taxi-cab drivers in London, who are required to memorize maps of the entire city to get their taxi-cab license have larger brain regions devoted to spatial or mapping memories.

Dr. Boyd goes on to say, "The third way your brain can support learning is by altering its function. As you engage a brain region, it becomes more and more excitable and easy to use again. As your brain has these areas that increase their excitability, the brain shifts how and when they are activated. In learning, it can be observed that whole networks of brain activity are shifting and changing.

Neuroplasticity is supported by chemical, structural and functional changes. Together they support learning and occur constantly.

The primary driver of change in your brain is your behavior. Patterns of neuroplasticity vary from person to person. Nothing is more effective than practice to help you learn. The bottom line is that you must do the work yourself. There's no pill you can take and no one else can do it for you. Behaviors that you employ in your everyday life are important, each of them changes your brain."

Dr. Boyd's research further demonstrates that increased difficulty or struggle during practice leads to more learning and greater structural changes to your brain. Your brain is tremendously plastic and is shaped, both structurally and functionally by everything you do and everything you don't do. You and your plastic brain are constantly being shaped by the world around you.

Understand that everything you encounter and everything you experience changes your brain. Repeat those behaviors that support a healthy personal security life style, and break those behaviors and habits that do not. Practice good personal security to build the brain you want – a brain that provides you comfort and protection in the new normal.

However, even if you live a personal security lifestyle, there are certain dedicated predators and opportunists who may force you into a black swan situation. If this happens, you still have two more options at your disposal – one of them is *active measures*, to affect the bad guy by denying his opportunity, and the other is *reactive measures* which is covered later.

Affect the Bad Guy

In U.S. criminal law, *means, motive,* and *opportunity* is a common summation of the three aspects of a crime that must be established before guilt can be determined in a criminal proceeding.

Respectively, they refer to: the ability of the perpetrator to commit the crime (means), the reason the perpetrator committed the crime (motive), and whether the perpetrator had the chance to commit the crime (opportunity). In defense against such an attack it is not possible to affect the bad guy's means or motive, but it is possible to affect the latter of the three – his *opportunity.*

A determined predator will use whatever means at his disposal, such as distraction techniques and the like, to carry out his plan of attack. However, for him to be successful, all he needs is an *opportunity.* Denying him that opportunity is what pulls the plug on his attack plans.

Breaking the cycle between the middle of step 3 (stalk) and all the way through step 4 (close), affords you the time and opportunity to affect the bad guy and the odds of you stopping the attack are still stacked in your favor.

Here's what you've got going for you: at mid-cycle you are in *Condition Orange* (Alert Mode) and alerted to the threat by identifying that threat, or threat indicator(s). You have limited options, less time and need a little more effort to execute *Active Measures.* However, you are afforded both the time and opportunity to affect the bad guy by denying him the opportunity. There are three ways to accomplish this task – what I call the three Ds of denying opportunity.

The first D is to *De-escalate* – If someone raises their voice and starts to get into a heated conversation with you and you realize that the pot of water is starting to, what are some things you can do to de-escalate the situation or lower the heat under the pot of water?

A 2016 controversial report by Washington, DC-based criminal justice think-tank the Police Executive Research Forum (PERF) lists 30 guiding principles for law enforcement use-of-force policy and training. At least eight of the guidelines directly mention de-escalation or discuss aspects of how officers can reduce force by backing off in situations where immediate action is not mandated by law or required for officer or public safety. Veteran street officers and trainers would tell you de-escalation is the result of a combination of communication, empathy, instinct, and sound officer safety tactics. And its goal is to help the officer achieve a good outcome where neither the officer nor the subject is injured[60].

Guiding principle # 18 of the 2016 PERF report, stresses the importance of effective communication[61]. Remaining in good communication with someone can include being aware of what the agitated person may be experiencing

---

60   Excerpt from Police Magazine article http://www.policemag.com/channel/careers-training/articles/2016/03/de-escalation-training-learning-to-back-off.aspx

61   http://www.policeforum.org/assets/guidingprinciples1.pdf

such as feelings, perspective, etc. from their point of view. Tuning into that person affords you a readable frequency from which to better communicate.

You can lower your voice, change your body language (present the palms of your hands), walk away, or any combination thereof.

The second "D" is to *Deter* – Armored glass[62], locks, alarms, live monitored video cameras, vetted access control and keeping your valuables out of plain sight, all contribute to deterring a would-be attacker. Each morning when you leave home you don't open every door and every window, blast loud music into the street and leave $100 bills all over the sidewalk out in front. No, you do the exact opposite to cause a burglar to consider your home too hard a target, and seek a much easier alternative.

The third D is to *Defuse*. Use verbal judo to find your way out. One of the best examples of defusing a situation is Antoinette Tuff who talked down an active shooter after he cranked off two rifle rounds into the foyer of an elementary school just outside Atlanta, Georgia and was in the process of pointing the muzzle in the direction of the kids. She was the only line of defense standing between the gunman and 800 children at that elementary school.

> Tuff watches as the gunman lowers the rifle and paces across the front office. He is a stocky man in his 20s with brown, cropped hair and a nose that looks like it's been broken. He is breathing heavily as he turns to Tuff and bellows: "Call

---

62   http://www.truarmor.com/glass-laminate/

911 and call a news station. Tell them I'm going to start shooting." Tuff's shaking hand grips the phone as she dials 911. She quickly complies with everything the gunman asks, addressing him as "sir" as she relays his messages to the dispatcher. The minutes drag on, and the gunman shouts threats and waves his rifle at Tuff. Tuff takes a risk. She asks the gunman an odd question: "Can I go to the bathroom?" The gunman stops pacing. He turns in her direction. The angry expression on his face evaporates.

Tuff's legs wobble as she rises to go to the bathroom. But before she can take another step, an awful thought comes to her: If I go to the bathroom, the gunman might follow, and I will inadvertently lead him to the classrooms where the children are hiding. By now Tuff knows the whole school has been warned over the school intercom that there is an intruder in the building. The teachers are keeping the children hidden in the classrooms. Tuff watches as the gunman takes a plastic chair from the office and uses it to prop open the school's main door. He raises his rifle and begins shooting at police, who by now have gathered outside.

Glass shatters and bullet casings scatter across the office. But for some reason, a blanket of calm settles over Tuff. She watches the gunman fire away, but doesn't move from her seat. Tuff takes another chance. "Sweetheart, come back in here,"

she tells the gunman. "Bullets don't have no
names. And those bullets gonna kill me and you.
I need you to come back in here and it's gonna
be you and me and we will work this thing out"[63].

Antoinette Tuff talked an active shooter into a cease fire
and defused a highly volatile situation which saved the
lives of all involved

What is the difference between de-escalate and defuse?
De-escalate means that something is starting to look like
it might get ugly and as things become more agitated
you can turn the heat down or off, before it boils over.
De-escalating a potential threat situation is like convinc-
ing someone to not follow through with their idea to put
a lit match to a bomb fuse. Defuse means that the bomb
fuse has already been lit. You have no choice but to cut
the fuse, to stop the imminent explosion.

Denying a bad guy his opportunity is nothing more than
taking active measures. It's about mitigating the threat
– making its impact less, or decreased. *Active measures*
may not be as optimal as *proactive measures*, but are
far better than the only remaining alternative, which is
reactive measures.

Failing proactive measures (eliminating soft target indicators), and active measures (denying the bad guy his
opportunity) – both of which mean you still have some
control over the threat using only soft skills, your only
remaining option is reactive measures. This is where things
have turned physical, and you are no longer in control of

---

63   http://www.cnn.com/2014/02/22/us/Tuff-survivor-gunman/

the threat. It's the last stage of a *threat progression* – to the right of bang, where you are relegated to physical response, using only your hard skills.

Affect the Process

Finding yourself at Step 5 of the *Attack Cycle* places you in *Condition Red* (Act Mode) and 100% reactive to the threat. In other words, the threat now controls you and you are tasked with regaining the initiative.

Having a natural aversion to pain, injury and death, the predator realizes that by personally, and physically, conducting an attack on another human being, he places himself at a great deal of risk. In plain speak, engaging in physical violence can raise the scale of injury to both predator and prey. It's a nagging burr ever present in the back of the predator's mind which causes him to continually ask himself the question "Are there softer targets?" You can take advantage of this natural predisposition by affecting the predator at Step 5.

Breaking the cycle at the very last step also means that you have the least amount of time, must exert the maximum amount of physical effort and are limited to only three remaining options. flight, fight or freeze.

Flight – Move off the X

Protection professionals such as military, law enforcement and protective agents are the highest-trained personnel in avoidance of, mitigation of and defense in personal combat. Failing avoidance and mitigation, and in the event of reacting to an active threat, if there ever was a magic bullet to ensure defense against an attack for them, it would be summed up in a single objective "Move off the X while sustaining the lowest *Scale of Injury*."

What is meant by moving off the X? The term was derived from back when they first started making movies. When filming, an actor stands on two pieces of tape placed on the floor in the shape of an X because that is the exact physical potion where the lights, cameras and microphones are focused.

The same concept applies in any physical threat – the bad guys and their guns, knives and bullets are all focused on that X. In any physical attack, when you *Move off the X* you are immediately getting yourself away from someplace bad and moving to a safer place.

We already know why sustaining the lowest *Scale of Injury* possible is a tactical consideration, so combining the two objectives; move of the X and with the lowest *Scale of Injury* provides you the very best hard skills solution to any active threat failing your soft skills (proactive and active measures).

The first and best reactive option in influencing the process (Step 5) is to move off the X otherwise known as "Flight." Whether in a vehicle (air, water or ground) or on foot, flight, brings you away from the threat, out of harm's way and with the least amount of physical injury – it is considered an optimal tactical response.

Fight – Do Whatever It Takes

Failing flight, the defensive A answer, your very next option is to use whatever physical means at your disposal to get yourself into a position so that you can get yourself out of danger and with the least amount of injury. The one-word description for this hard skill is to fight.

Fighting is not easy. Fighting is not Pretty. Fighting is pure violence of action. It transcends all language and cultural barriers. It requires full mental and physical commitment. It may be throwing a hammer at his head or a scalding hot pot of coffee in his face or slamming a pair of scissors into your attacker's left eye to cause a distraction. Whatever it takes to immediately fight your way out is always better than the alternative.

Either you control the fight, or the fight controls you. There are no other options. Your primary objective, when it comes down to physical violence, is to take the initiative by any means necessary. In the world of physical violence, there are countless ways you can be hurt or killed. Explosive devices, firearms, hazardous materials, moving vehicles, edged and impact weapons, to name a few, have been used in the past, and will continue to be used well into the foreseeable future.

Aside from being hit with chemical, biological, nuclear, radioactive or explosive devices, from which there are no immediate reactive measures, (these are best handled left of bang), and as covered earlier, the two general categories of weapons that can raise your *Scale of Injury* are ballistic (firearms) and non-ballistic weapons (edged, impact, and flexible weapons).

Defending Your Personal Battle Space

In the event of an active threat, your personal battle space can span from hundreds of yards to conversational ranges. These can be divided into three discernable distances – ballistic long range (sniper), ballistic close quarters and non-ballistic ranges. Defending your personal battle space depends on what distance and weapon(s) used by your attacker(s).

Sniper Defense

At long range, a sniper can hit you from viable distances determined by the capability of the attacker and their weapon system. Long gunners, using a rifle, can strike far beyond or outside your line of sight using extreme distance, concealment, position[64], camouflage, etc., which means you may not be able to see them. Your defensive options at long range and under these extreme conditions, are to identify the impact area, and immediately seek cover[65]. Use your sensory input to confirm that it is gunfire. Take that golden tenth of a second to orient to the direction of incoming rounds as you do not want to inadvertently run into a hailstorm of flying lead.

Crowded public areas have proven to be attractive targets for terrorist, predators and opportunists alike. According to former US Marine and retired SWAT team commander (and sniper) for Lake County Sherriff's Office (Illinois),

---

64   https://www.washingtonpost.com/news/morning-mix/wp/2017/10/02/
     police-shut-down-part-of-las-vegas-strip-due-to-shooting/?utm_
     term=.358cd984b39f
65   Cover is anything of substantial thickness or material durable enough to
     stop a rifle round, such as a concrete wall or steel column.

Tom Rovetuso of Angel One Training, LLC, and other operators, there are five proactive measures you can take if you are considering attending a very large public gathering (concert, sporting event, etc.)

1. Don't go. The very simple and easy proactive measure to avoid being shot by a sniper at a large-scale event, is don't show up. If you don't show up for a mass-shooting, then there's a 100% guarantee that you will not be shot. However, as Dr. Bucci mentioned in his foreword do you really want to stay behind closed doors and live in fear? No. So there are at least four other proactive measures you can take.

2. If you go, then position yourself and those with you, nearest readily accessible cover and/ or exit points. Using cover and/ or egressing from an impact area is relative to your proximity to them. The closer you are to those hard points[66], the less time it takes for you to use them. The further away you are, the longer the distance you must travel, which increases the amount of time you are exposed to danger.

3. Should you need to go hard and fast mobile, (dodge sniper fire), then you need to move as quickly as you are able. Physical disabilities, injuries, or wearing restrictive clothing can hamper your mobility/ speed. Tight clothing, high heels, loose flip flops, etc., can affect your movement. It is recommended that you wear footwear and clothing that will allow you to run at least 500 yards across a parking lot, through traffic,

---

66 Hard Point is professional protection parlance for "a space safer than from where you are running." Typically, a hard point can be cover, concealment, an area out of threat reach, or all above.

a train station, or a shopping mall.

4. It's also a good idea to always have a compact bleeding/ gunshot-wound trauma kit (to include a tourniquet) on hand. Stopping the blood flow is one of the most important steps you can take in treating a gunshot or shrapnel wound. Keeping a few medical supplies on hand could save your life, or the life of another. Mike McBee, SMSgt USAF ACC 58 RQS/OPS, recommends a basic gunshot wound (GSW) trauma kit to include a tourniquet, combat gauze, control elastic wrap, chest seal and a space blanket. The form/ size of your kit should be a factor in your consideration. Is it compact enough for everyday carry? Will you carry it in your purse, in your car, keep one at your office? Bottom line w/ a GSW kit is to win the fight, "stop the bleed, help them breathe, warm not freeze and get ready to leave."

5. When you know you're going to an event that may be considered an attractive target, then appropriately adjust your personal security radar, set your baseline and enjoy the show!

Close Quarters Defense

In the case of an active shooter in a confined area (not a sniper), who is moving on foot, there are a few more defensive options at your disposal than those limited by sniper fire. As covered earlier, the very best way to stop an active shooter is a trained shooter with a firearm. Any less use of force, is less than optimal. Unarmed defense against an active shooter is the least effective defensive response. However, if that's all you've got to work with, then you still

have "Run, Hide, Fight" which remain the most tradition-
ally viable unarmed defensive options to date.

Getting off the X is your very best option when you know
where the attack is, and you know where you're going. In
doing so, you create distance between yourself and the
attacker. You also remain a moving target, which always
more difficult to hit than a stationary one.

However, you may not be able to run because of physical
impairment(s), or you may have young children with
you who cannot keep up, the power is out and to run is
hazardous, as mentioned earlier you're wearing restrictive
clothing or footwear, or your runway puts you directly in
the path, or proximity of the killer.

Running for cover is always the very best option but if you
cannot, then you have the concealment option – temporarily hidden from the killer's direct line of sight. Unlike
cover, concealment will not stop bullets, but you can also
use cover for concealment.

If you're forced into having no other option, such as you're
unable to run or fight to due physical impairment, you
would be best served hiding in a hard room that can be
effectively barricaded and locked (from the inside) with a
good deadbolt. Your optimal hiding place is one with an
escape route where you may need a temporary delay or
maneuver to buy you time because you know the cavalry
is on the way.

Stop the Threat

Aside from taking flight, the next recommended option is to stop the threat. Being unarmed places you at an extreme tactical disadvantage but not an impossible one.

Time is a critical factor, as the greatest number of casualties usually occur in the first five minutes. Don't delay – take him down fast. You will have several opportunities to accomplish this task, when:

- He is within arm's reach
- His finger is not on trigger
- His weapon is not ready
- He is reloading
- There is a lull in the action
- He is distracted (shouting, talking, etc.)
- He's moving
- There is a mechanical or shooter malfunction
- He sets down or drops his weapon
- Your lockdown has been breached
- You can set up an effective ambush

You can take him down with projectile weapons (throw chairs, tables, scalding hot pots of coffee at him), propellants such as hair spray or wasp spray (add a lighter for more affect), impact weapons (baseball bat, closet dowel, rolling pin, frying pan), edged weapons (scissors or steak knife in the eye), flexible weapon (purse strap, belt, computer cable) around the neck (break, asphyxiate, choke), your bare hands, elbows or knees and overwhelming force (a large group of people rushing him) slamming him into a wall or launching him down a flight of stairs.

Mechanical Compliance

When it comes down to a stopping a physical threat, there are only two ways you can control your opponent(s). Your options are either *pain compliance* or *mechanical compliance.*

The least effective of the two is *pain compliance* as everyone has a different threshold of pain tolerance. You can punch some guy right in the kisser as hard as you possibly can and he might just stand there completely unaffected and smile at you. The reasons for this may be that he's under the influence of drugs or alcohol or that he's physically conditioned or that he's just a really tough guy with a super-high pain tolerance.

Mechanical compliance, on the other hand, affords you the very best option in any physical altercation. If you cut a guy's biceps or Achilles tendon with a knife, or make accurate rifle round placement to the head, then it doesn't matter how tough-guy he may be as body mechanics and physics trump pain tolerance.

Using *mechanical compliance* over *pain compliance* will serve you best in stopping a killer. When it comes to an active shooter, you are not required to stop the threat by law, but always consider the alternative – you stop him, or he kills you.

Non-Ballistic Defense

An attacker wielding any non-ballistic weapon such as a knife or a baseball bat, requires physical contact between the attacker(s) and yourself to be effective in raising your *Scale of Injury* which require additional defensive options.

Reactionary Gap

In the first play of a baseball game the pitcher throws the ball to the batter who smacks it way out into left field. The outfielder sees the hit, watches the ball, has plenty of time to prepare, set up for and complete his catch. The very next play the pitcher throws the same pitch, this time the batter drills the ball straight toward the pitcher who barely had time to duck out of the way.

The difference between the two plays is the amount of time the outfielder and pitcher had to react. The same physics applies to an active threat. The less the space between you and the threat, the less time you have to react; conversely the greater the space, the greater the amount of reaction time. This concept is known as the *Reactionary Gap.*

Two guys standing toe-to-toe with guns blazing are eventually going to get hurt or killed. Two guys with a knife toe-to-toe slashing and hacking away at each other are eventually going to meet the same fate as the gun guys.

In personal combat, time is a critical factor. The longer you wait to control the fight, the deeper you fall into the rabbit hole, as it becomes increasingly more difficult to take control. The quicker you take control of the situation, the greater your odds on keeping control, and gaining the initiative to move yourself and those with you to safety.

Two in Two

In a non-ballistics weapons attack, if you must fight your way out quickly as possible. Time is not on your side. More time on the X increases your potential for personal injury. Your goal in fighting your way out from between a rock and a hard place to a position where you can take flight, is to make every physical movement count and keep these moves to a minimum. The optimal is two moves or less.

The first two seconds of any gunfight regardless of distance are the most critical. A military-age male between the ages of 18 and 32 wielding a non-ballistic weapon, can close the distance of ten yards (30 feet) in approximately 1.5 seconds (just under 2 seconds). Therefore, anything more than two moves in two seconds is too much time and will not serve you. Your best defensive results occur with the least amount of movement in the shortest amount of time. Two moves in two seconds, or as I have coined the phrase: two-in-two (2N2).

Control the Fight

Taking control of anything means that you must first gain control what makes that thing work. For example, controlling a car means that you control the steering wheel, the brake pedal and the gas pedal. Losing control of any one or all three of these devices would result in your losing control of the vehicle. Conversely, gaining control of all three devices allows you control of the vehicle.

The same applies to controlling a fight. There are three "devices" that you can identify and gain control of in any violent physical altercation. To do this, you must first gain control of your immediate environment. To do this, you need to control the time and space around you.

We know from *Reactionary Gap*, the more space you have, the more time you have, to react; the less space there is to work with, the less time you have, to react. More time and more space afford you more options and greater opportunities. Less time and less space gives you less options and less opportunity to solve the tactical problem. A valuable personal security formula is derived from this equation:

More space = more time = more opportunity to solve the tactical problem.

The converse is also true:

Less space = less time = less opportunity to solve the tactical problem.

You gain control over your opponent(s) by gaining more opportunities, which you get by gaining more space, which buys you more time. You can accomplish this by taking control of the three devices integral to any physical altercation: distance, position and movement.

Controlling Distance

The first of the three is *Distance* – how far away you are from the threat. It is the measurement of space between yourself and your attacker(s). In non-ballistic defense, this space can be measured by two references: contact range (without moving his feet if he can reach out with either arm and cut you with a knife, smack you with a bat, grab your arm or punch you in the face) and non-contact range where he is standing at least an arm and one-half length away from you or more where he cannot physically contact you (where it would require him to move his feet to reach you).

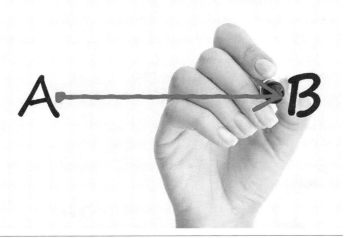

Fig. 21. Distance is the measurement from Point "A" to point "B"

At *Non-contact Range*, you have more distance at your disposal. We know from the *Reactionary Gap*, that more distance equals more time. More time and more distance afford you more options and greater opportunity. In addition to these tremendous benefits of being out of reach of your opponent(s), you are also at the very bottom of the *Scale of Injury*, which is level zero, with no injury. Given all the above, Non-contact range is the best possible scenario and is the safest of the two ranges.

Injury Distance Relationship

Conversely, moving so close to your opponent that they can make physical contact with you means you are now at *Contact Range* - where injury begins.

As there exists a relationship between time and space, there exists a relationship between distance and injury. The further away the lower your injury. The closer he gets to you the greater your potential for sustaining grave bodily injury or perhaps death.

Imagine a guy with a knife. At the very onset of *Contact Range*, he can just barely clip your fingertip (level one on the *Scale of Injury*) but if he took one step closer and cut your biceps now you've gone up to level two. One step closer and he can now put the knife to your throat which takes you to level four. This example illustrates the distance-injury relationship. Distance is your friend and you want to place as much of it as possible between yourself and your attacker(s). The relationship between distance and *Scale of Injury* is like the relationship between distance and reaction time. The closer he gets to you the greater your potential for a raised *Scale of Injury*. The greater distance you keep with your assailant(s) the lower your potential for injury with a non-ballistic weapon. *Contact Range* begins where injury is possible.

Distance is Your Friend

Moving away from the threat you have increased space, which buys you time which buys you more tactical options. Using a technique, I call "the *Nike™ Defense*" is to simply point your heels toward the threat and run! The greater the distance, the greater your options. However, it's not always possible to put space between yourself and the threat. Your next best bet is to place objects between yourself and the threat. Obstructions such as cars, trees, trash cans, your ex-wife's attorney, furniture, mailbox, etc.

Force your attacker(s) to move around them which in turn buys you more time to make more distance. More time and more space buy you more options, including getting yourself off the X and to a safe place.

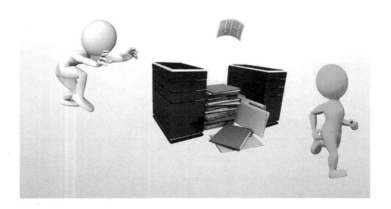

Fig. 22. Obstructions buy you more time

Creating more space to include using obstructions buys you more time. The *Nike™ Defense* works great in open spaces such a parking garages, open outdoor plazas, in a mall, etc. However, these options may not be available to you in certain situations. Engaging a threat in confined areas such as crowded restaurants, hallways, stairways, elevators, etc., presents a problem when creating space (or using obstructions) is not an option. If you cannot change the distance from your threat you can change your physical location or *position* relative to that threat. This is the second component of controlling any fight at non-ballistic ranges.

Controlling Position

Imagine you are standing directly in front of your opponent with a knife in his hand at conversational distance. We call this Position Zero which is not a very good place to be because you're already at contact range and he's got a knife in one hand, he can punch or grab you with his other hand, deliver elbows knees round-kicks and a head butt and all without the need to move his feet.

Most law enforcement professionals are taught to move to Position One which, although still at contact range, is to align your belt buckle with his left arm. This is a more advantageous position, because it negates the reach of his right arm and right leg, Position One is the standard as taught to law enforcement professionals for conducting field interviews.

Fig. 23. Change your physical position relative to the threat

Moving forward, standing directly next to your attacker facing his left shoulder is labeled Position Two as this puts you in an even more advantageous position. Ultimately, the dominant position in any fight is getting to your attacker's back or Position Three which places you directly behind your attacker facing the back of his head. This is exactly opposite of Position Zero. Position Three is the best physical position you can be in any fight.

If you cannott change your distance from the threat or use obstructions, then at least place yourself in a position of advantage. The lower your physical position (Position Zero) relative to the threat the greater your *Scale of Injury*. The higher the position (Position Three) relative to your threat, the lesser your *Scale of injury*. The concept here is to fight for the higher numbers.

Controlling Mobility

To change either distance or position you need to be move. Stay mobile. A moving target is always more difficult to hit than a stationary target. Someone chasing you down swinging a baseball bat will have a *much* more difficult time contacting your melon if you keep moving and changing direction.

If people were chasing after you trying to cut your head off, you'd probably want to move as fast as you can. The best way to do that is to first be stable.

Located just down Exeter Road from where I teach up at Sig Sauer Academy, a shooting range in Epping New Hampshire, is the New England Drag Way. Some of the fastest NHRA[67] cars run on that track. Those speedy cars have the biggest and widest tires. Why? The answer is to make as much contact with the track as possible. To achieve maximum speed, you need stability. Look at any rocket or aircraft. To reach their necessary speeds they need fixed or stable wings.

We as humans have neither wide tires nor fixed wings. However, we do have legs and feet that can be made stable. If you look at some of the very best boxers in history, such as Sugar Ray Robinson, and Muhammed Ali, they were rock-solid on their feet yet could move quickly and deliver powerful effective strikes. How did they do that? By building and moving a stable fighting platform.

---

67   The National Hot Rod Association, the largest auto racing organization in the world

Stable Fighting Platform

One of my Filipino Martial Arts Masters, Punong Guro Edgar Sulite, founder of the LAMECO system of Eskrima, taught that controlling your balance was critical to your survival in non-ballistic defense. He said to beware of your attacker(s) taking your balance. "If they take from you your balance, they may then take from you your life." The military teaches to keep your enemies off balance.

Balance is critical and to have good balance means a solid defensive foundation. Building your stable fighting platform, like building a house, starts with a concrete foundation. Set your feet flat on the ground (maximum contact equals maximum control) about shoulder-width apart and directly under your hips. All ten toes can be touching the same imaginary line of demarcation or you can have your dominant foot's toes along a line perpendicular to the instep of your non-dominant foot. Either configuration will set a strong foundation.

If you lock your legs completely straight and someone asked you to move left or right what's the very first thing you'd need to do? Yes, unlock your knees so that you could be readily mobile.

The next step in building your foundation is to redistribute your weight slightly forward onto the balls of your feet as if you were preparing to push open an extremely large, heavy door.

In this position, your feet firmly contacting the ground shoulder-width apart, knees unlocked, and toes covered by your knees which should be covered by your chin (weight slightly forward) you have built a solid foundation. This is all good for below your belt, but what about your hands? Where should they go?

Since prehistorical times when the first caveman slapped the second cave man, man has learned the hard way, how to raise his hands up in protection of his most vital upper body vulnerable target – his neck.

The neck is a conduit for the hydraulics (circulatory system) for which fluids must move upward through the neck to get to the brain. The neck is also a conduit for air (pneumatics) to get from the nose and mouth and into the lungs. Thirdly, it is an electrical conduit for the computer to send signals via the nervous system to other body parts. Cut or crush the conduit and you shut down any one or possibly all three systems – hydraulics, pneumatics and electrical.

Your forearms are used to protect the conduit from damage. Keeping your elbows pointing down can help protect your rib cage and some internal organs. Your hands can be either in Ready Position or Defense Position.

Much like a field interview position (law enforcement) Ready Position is where the officer keeps his/ her hands open and moving above the belt placing a barrier between themselves and a potential threat, but in a relaxed position. In this position your hands are relaxed enough to gesture with them if you want. Although you may perceive no imminent danger, having your hands in the relaxed ready position affords you a rapid and effective unarmed response option. They place a natural obstruction between you and a potential threat.

When speaking with anyone you may have your doubts about, at conversational ranges (contact distance – where injury begins), it's a good idea to casually move to position one, keep your knees unlocked, weight slightly forward, ready to move (know where you will move – have a plan) and your hands up in ready position assisting with your conversation.

Defensive position is where your hands are formed into closed fists and you've switched from Ready Position to protection of your conduit with the outside of your forearms facing the threat who has initiated the attack. Better to take a knife slash against the outside of your forearm than your exposed neck. Keep in mind that personal injury is a tactical consideration.

Raising your hands up (palms facing you) to about cheekbone level, much like a boxer (keeping your elbows pointed down to protect your ribs) creates a natural barrier between incoming strikes and your all-important upper-body conduit. You don't want to cover your eyes with your hands because if you lose sight you'll lose the fight!

If you keep that solid foundation and those hands up in either Ready or Defensive Position, you have built a stable fighting platform.

Moving the Stable Fighting Platform

Now that you've built the platform you need to move it – quickly. There are two ways you can do that. You can either walk-step (one foot in front of the other) which most of us should have down pretty good by now so I don't want to spend much time on that, and the other is a shuffle step – or a big step, followed by a little step. Rule of thumb for moving the stable fighting platform with the shuffle step is to first move the foot nearest the direction you want to move. If you've never done it, try step and slide right, left, forward and backward on for size.

The advantages, at contact range in non-ballistic defense, of the shuffle step are that it's short, explosive and very powerful, the disadvantage is that it's slow moving. The pro to the walk step is that it's fast. The con is that it's not stable. In the world of fight control, you need to be comfortable with both.

Next time you find yourself in a casual conversation, stand in position one, knees unlocked, weight slightly forward, in a stable fighting platform ready to mobilize with hands up waiving around helping you with the discussion – none of it offensive – but, all of it giving you the tactical advantage of being prepared to engage an *active threat* should things break bad.

Get In or Get out

When you disengage from a non-ballistic weapons attack, you have completed your 2N2 and now you must pick a direction in which to move off the X – either create space (Get Out) by stepping back and away at a 45 degree angle, or change your position relative to the threat (Get In) by fighting for the higher numbers, moving to Position Three. You can get in quickly by stepping 45 degrees to Position Two or even Position Three in one or two rapid shuffle steps. Given two positions to Get Out and two positions to Get In, you have a grand total of four positions total to where you can move from Position Zero or off the X.

The safest of these is to Get Out as more space lowers your potential for injury and provides you more time which buys you more opportunity to solve the tactical problem. If given a choice, or when in doubt, Get Out.

Exit or Equalize

Even with a fast-moving stable fighting platform, you are at a horrific disadvantage with your bare hands versus an attacker swinging a knife, machete or tire iron at your head. If you can't get off the X, immediately get something in your hands. It can be a book, your backpack, a trash can, a rolled-up jacket – anything that can protect you from that contact weapon. Even if you need to smack the knife away with your bare hands and move, don't just stand there on the "X" and wait for your *Scale of Injury* to raise. Your end goal is to keep moving until you can either create enough space and time to take flight or gain access to a superior position by fighting for the higher numbers.

Exiting is always your very best option. If not possible, you will be challenged with use of force by way of one or more armed attackers. Unable to exit, your only remaining option is to get something in your hands to equalize the force being used against you. Getting something in your hands, means anything that's not anchored to the ground that you can lift high enough to use in self-defense against your assailant(s) with the purpose of stopping or temporarily immobilizing them so that you can get off that X and get to safety. Your very best bet is to reach for a weapon of opportunity or improvised weapon instantly accessible to you, and in your immediate environment.

Improvised Weapons

A non-ballistic or improvised weapon can be any object not nailed to the floor. It can be anything that is made of metal, wood, plastic, glass, wire or any other material capable of holding an edge, point or rigidity that can be used in self-defense to stop a violent physical attack.

Non-ballistic weapons can be grouped into four general categories:

1. Edged Weapons
2. Impact Weapons
3. Flexible Weapons
4. Personal Weapons

Category 1 – Edged Weapons. Includes knives, razor blades, nails, sharpened credit cards, pens, scissors, pencils, broken glass, coat hanger, kitchen utensils, screwdrivers and any object with an edge or a point that can cut or puncture. Category 1 is the most versatile as the edge and tip are two surface areas of a non-ballistic weapon that can be applied in the same attack and *at the same time.* No other type of improvised weapon can claim this dual-function capability.

Category 2 - Impact weapons. Includes broom handles, baseball bats, telephones, tire irons, lumber, ax handles, thick or high heel shoes, rocks, tree branches, pipes, sticks, toilet plunger handles, closet dowels, crowbars and the like which can shatter bone. This is the second most effective category as these weapons can cause structural damage and render your assailant(s) incapacitated by impact alone.

Category 3 - Flexible weapons. Includes computer cable, rope, piano wire, belt, bungee cord, silk scarf, telephone cord, purse strap, chain, trash can liner and any object with flexibility -anything that can be used to either establish a choke hold, asphyxiation or crush the trachea. Although not as common as the categories of edged and impact weapons, this category of improvised weapons demands an equal level of respect. The number one form of prisoner execution in the United States up until 1936 was hanging by rope - a flexible weapon – until dead.

Category 4 - Personal weapons. Includes fists, knees, fingernails, shins, elbows, head butts, stomping, biting and any body part that can emulate the functionality of edged, impact or flexible weapons and inflict physical damage. It's far easier to stop a threat with an edged, impact or flexible weapon than it is with the bottom of your shoes, but it can be done.

To effectively employ a non-ballistic weapon from any category, you must first be able to identify and then use it to give you the decisive advantage in a violent physical encounter. What must you know to identify, access and effectively deploy every-day items in your environment to defend yourself if necessary? It all starts with a *Resource Assessment Listing*. This is nothing more than a mental checklist created by you internally, on the fly, when you are faced with a potential threat. You walk into a room and identify any loose accessible item you can instantly grasp with your bare hands that, upon your rapid consideration, meet all three criteria: 1. Proximity – the nearer to you the better. You may even need to move closer to it. 2. Speed – how quickly can you get it into your hand? Is it heavy, light, compact, clumsy? 3. Deployable – how effectively can this object be utilized in self-defense as a non-ballistic weapon? For example, a pillow as an impact weapon (Category 2) is probably not your best choice.

Let's take a minute to run a cognitive visualization training exercise. Take a walk with your mind's eye into your kitchen and identify an edged weapon. Where is it? Where would you need to be standing so that you could get it in either hand? How quickly could you do this? Can it be used effectively in self-defense as a non-ballistic weapon to stop the threat? Next scan the same room again using your mind's eye and identify an impact weapon. Where is it? Where would you need to be standing so that you could get it in either hand? How quickly could you do this? Can it be used effectively in self-defense as a non-ballistic weapon to stop the threat? Next scan the room again using your mind's eye and identify a flexible weapon. Where is it? Where would you need to be standing so that you could get it in either hand? How quickly could you do this? Can it be used effectively in self-defense as a non-ballistic weapon to stop the threat? Lastly, of all three categories (edged, impact, flexible) which one do you think would be the very best option to stop a physical threat?

The next level of your training is to run a *Resource Assessment Listing* at work, a restaurant, a business meeting or dinner party. Nobody else needs to know what you're doing. Just smile and figure out how to stop a threat if you had to with what was made available to you in your immediate environment.

Running a resource assessment listing can give you the tactical advantage you need when there are no other options. Your ability to run a *Resource Assessment Listing* is an exceptional soft skill that you can keep in your proverbial tool kit should the need arise.

Deploying a non-ballistic weapon, is simply a matter of picking up the readily-accessible weapon of opportunity with your hand(s) and immediately applying it to the nearest bad guy.

Your objective is not to take on single or multiple assailants who themselves may be armed, because there may be more of them than there are of you. He/ they may be younger, harder, stronger, faster and have done more time behind bars than you.

Your objective is to do what it takes to make him react. This can be by distraction, redirection, resistance or even feigned compliance. You only need to read the need. The desired end result is to buy yourself enough time, space and opportunity to get out. As covered earlier the formula to take control of any fight:

1. Bad guy has the action-reaction power curve
2. Good guy causes bad guy to react (using non-ballistic weapon)
3. Good guy takes action-reaction power curve

Should you ever find yourself between a rock and a hard place, you now have another viable option up your sleeve that can give you the tactical advantage. Better to have and not need, than to need and not have. Think of this life-saving information as layers of protection insulating yourself and your family from the effects of a violent physical attack.

Regardless of how you fight to make your attacker(s) react, your immediate next move is to take flight. Get off that X with the least amount if injury to yourself and those with you as quickly as you can. Remember to exit or equalize![68]

Freeze – Surrender to Your Attacker(s)

Failing flight or fight, you have only one remaining option and that is to submit to your attacker(s) – surrender. This is not optimal, but you always have a choice. Which of the three is the safest? The answer is flight or fight (followed by flight) – why? Because it takes you out of harm's way, and decreases your potential for physical injury, which, if may you recall, is a tactical consideration. The least advisable is to freeze because you are subjected to the whims of terrorists, criminals, opportunists and predators.

Which one will you choose? If you are trained and know how and where to escape or take flight, then the odds of survival are stacked in your favor. If you're trained in hard skills (firearms, edged weapons, boxing, ground fighting,

---

68   Exit or Equalize is a term coined by martial arts icon Guro Dan Inosanto in Los Angeles CA in the late 1980's.

etc.,) then you pose a persistent problem for your attacker(s) as throughout the fight they will be constantly asking the question "Are there softer targets?" and considering the answer to be "Yes."

Staying in good physical condition (running, endurance, etc.,), mental conditioning (developing your mental toughness) and having other hard skills (boxing, ground fighting, etc.,) only stack the odds in your favor and provide you with more effective physical response options should things move to the right of bang.

Finding yourself to the right of bang you are relegated to relying solely upon your hard skills. Reliance on only your hard skills is a very bad place to be.

You may realistically find yourself up against a wall, with no remaining options but flight, fight or freeze. In contrast, it truly makes a compelling argument for the benefits of using proactive and active measures.

Potential Threat	Active Threat	Step 1 Look	Step 2 Choose	VERIFY	Step 3 Stalk	PLAN	Step 4 Close	Step 5 Attack

The 90% Advantage						10%
Soft Skills						Hard Skills
Proactive Measures				Active Measures		Reactive Measures
Avoid				Mitigate		Defend
Unlimited Options				Limited Options		Three Options: Flight, Fight or Freeze
Maximum Amount of Time				Less Time		Least Time
Least Amount of Effort				More Effort		Max Effort

Fig. 24. Defeating an Attack: Proactive,
Active and Reactive Measures

PART IV

HOW TO CONTROL FEAR

CHAPTER 10

CONTROLLING FEAR

> ## "Men are disturbed not by things, but by the view they take of them."
> ### EPICTETUS (55-135AD)

A common question that rears its ugly head when things get physically violent is: What about fear? When it really matters, how do you manage your fear? There are many approaches to an optimal solution. One of these is analyzing fear from multiple perspectives, providing you a greater understanding of what it is, how it functions and, more specifically, how to control it.

According to Webster's Merriam Dictionary[69], fear is a word that can be used as either a noun or a verb. Used as

---

69   http://www.merriam-webster.com/dictionary/fear

a noun, fear is defined as "an unpleasant emotion caused by the belief that someone or something is dangerous, likely to cause pain, or a threat." Used as a verb, it means to "be afraid of (someone or something) as likely to be dangerous, painful, or threatening."

Fear, from a psychological perspective, is defined as a vital response to physical and emotional danger. If we didn't feel it, we couldn't protect ourselves from legitimate threats[70]. Fear is an emotional response induced by a perceived threat, which causes a change in brain and organ function, as well as in behavior.

Fear, from a physiological perspective, is primitive. In the wild, it instinctively protects animals from predators, but for humans, the emotion can be far more complex. Fear can trigger the 'fight or flight' response to raise the heart rate, sharpen the senses and provide access to huge amounts of energy to cope with threats to survival.

Neurologically speaking, the periaqueductal gray, or PAG, is an area of gray matter found in the midbrain. The PAG surrounds the cerebral aqueduct (hence the name periaqueductal) and occupies a column of brainstem that stretches about 14 mm long.

According to neuroscientists, the PAG appears to play a part in the regulation of heart rate and blood pressure, and it is thought that the PAG may help to adjust cardiovascular activity in the context of emotional experiences. The PAG also seems to contribute to many other autonomic

---

70   https://www.psychologytoday.com/basics/fear

processes, and it is important to the control and contraction of the bladder in humans and other animals.

The PAG also seems to be involved with emotional responses. It appears to be especially likely to be influential in the production of fearful and defensive reactions, as stimulation of the PAG can elicit these types of reactions in a variety of animals; human participants also displayed activation of the PAG when a threat came closer to them.[71]

Fear, from the philosophical perspective, like any other human emotion, such as happiness or sadness, is experienced by all people regardless of ethnicity, religion, gender, or political affiliation. Some may have a fear of heights, others may have a fear of closed spaces, and still others may have a fear of public speaking. Regardless of what may trigger the emotion, fear is made manifest by a perceived idea (conceptual) of an active threat (physical).

Normalcy Bias is very different than fear. *Normalcy Bias* is a psychological phenomenon that causes your mind to reinterpret dangerous events and assure you that everything is OK when things are not OK. It can make you stare with a smile at an active threat. But, it can also be defeated as covered earlier. Fear can impact your performance physiologically, and induce the three - flight/ fight (optimal) or freeze (less than optimal) defensive responses. Fear can be both actively and proactively controlled.

---

71   http://www.neuroscientificallychallenged.com/blog/know-your-brain-periaqueductal-gray

Frozen with Fear

At times, your perception of a threat may be so intense that it could cause a 'freeze' response. This could be interpreted as the brain being overwhelmed, or it may have evolved as a way of keeping still to hide from predators. Either way, neuroscientists have discovered how the brain links its survival circuits to the spinal cord, causing the body to freeze in the face of danger[72]. Regardless of the biomechanics, bottom line is when facing a real-world violent physical threat, you could literally freeze in your tracks. If you should find yourself in this situation, what can you do to rapidly thaw? Hailing from the world of Tier One Government (T1G) assets[73] running special operations, we are presented with the top two – breathing and humor.

Take a Breather

Controlled breathing has been the practice of yogis and monks for thousands of years. It has been proven over millennia in traditional practices to support meditation, blood flow, motivation and overall human performance.

On one of my OCONUS[74] assignments, I recall stepping off an aircraft and realizing we were all in a very precarious situation on the ground. I froze up for a split second. Looking at the operators around me who also realized the

---

72   http://www.dailymail.co.uk/sciencetech/article-2612117/Scared-stiff-
      Scientists-discover-brain-sends-signals-make-freeze-faced-danger.
      html#ixzz4pHQ6iWu6
73   US Department of Defense special operations community personnel such as
      Army Special Forces and Navy SEALs
74   Outside the Continental United States (OCONUS)

severity of our condition, all in the same freeze position, I observed each one of them take a huge deep breath, so I immediately followed suit. It brought us all out of the fog and we were all able to move forward. A deep cleansing breath, clears your mind and allows you to focus on the job at hand. Look at any serious competitor. Before they step into that ring, up to the plate or in the arena, what's the very last thing they do before high-demand performance? They take that same deep cleansing breath. If taking that thawing breath works for T1Gs and world-class competitors when it really counts, there's a very good chance it may work for you!

Crack a Joke

Army Special Forces and Navy SEALs concur that one of the most effective ways to deal with fear is to find the humor and laugh about it. As one operator puts it, laughter lets him consciously know that everything is "It's all going to work out."

There is recent evidence to back this up. A Stanford University study[75] revealed that people who were trained to make jokes in response to disturbing images dealt with them in a much healthier way than those who weren›t given the chance. Laughing in the face of fear made fear run away in embarrassment. The new normal is filled with twists and turns of the unexpected, and seeing the funny side of it can make living in it a lot easier.

---

75   http://news.stanford.edu/news/2011/august/humor-coping-horror-080111.
      html

Manage Fear Proactively

Rather than wait to *react* to a physiological response such as freezing, how much more of a tactical advantage is it to positively influence the effects of fear *before* you find yourself with your mouth open, staring at the white elephant. What are some things you can do to *proactively* manage your fear? You can change your perspective and manage your expectations.

You can't control everything that comes your way, but you are in absolute control of how you can *react* to it. The Greek philosopher Epictetus said, "Men are disturbed not by things, but the view they take of them."[76] Philosophically speaking, you can change your perspective which in turn will change your reality.

Know what to expect. A boxer expects to get hit in the face with the gloves of his opponent. A police officer expects to arrest law-breaking subjects, and a firefighter expects to put out a raging blaze. Each of these professionals is conditioned, inoculated, and accustomed to these anticipated threats. The same applies to protection professionals, who are trained to expect the unexpected and are prepared to handle it.

You have more control than you may think. You can't control what happens in the outside world, but you can control your interpretation of it. Developing skills and confidence in how you react to certain stimuli is the key to success in controlling fear.

---

76   Greek Stoic Philosopher (55-135AD) who travelled from Turkey and taught in ancient Rome and Greece

Philosophically speaking, if someone asked you, "*Are* you your job or do you *have* a job?" You would most likely respond that you *have* a job. You therefore, are not your job. You exist separate from your job. If someone asked you "Do you *have* emotions or *are* you your emotions?" you would most likely respond that you *have* (or experience) emotions. You are therefore *not* your emotions. You exist separate from your emotions.

Separating yourself from your emotions is something that many professionals have learned throughout their respective careers. Although everyone experiences fear during their lifetime, some people find emotional detachment more readily accessible than others. Realizing that you *allow* yourself to experience fear will allow you to detach from your emotions, specifically separating yourself from the fear emotion.

Psychologically speaking, you can become inoculated to fear using familiarization. As a federally certified firearms instructor it was my responsibility to take people who had never fired a gun before, and make them not only safe, but also able to pass a basic firearms qualification. Many students knew nothing about guns, and as such, were deathly afraid of them.

Taking them into a classroom and using non-functioning firearm replicas, I ran them through the fundamentals of shooting, a brief history of firearms, how the handgun functions and eventually placed a replica in their hands so they became familiarized with its weight, feel, and function. Their fear levels dropped exponentially as they gained greater familiarization.

Like the body becoming inoculated by introducing a small amount of the vaccine and inducing a natural chemical reaction, the mind will react to familiarizing itself in such a manner as to cause a psychological inoculation.

When someone tells you a good joke for the very first time, you laugh out loud and slap your knee because it was so funny. Then you hear it again, and it's not as funny so maybe you half-heartedly snicker. The next time you hear the very same joke you're pretty much over it and you may politely smile. These same mechanics apply to fear. The more you experience the same thing repeatedly, the more desensitized you become to that thing. One of the best ways to practice experiencing fear is to visualize a dreaded situation that literally makes your palms sweat.

Back in my youth, when I was a rock climber, I had a healthy fear of heights and although having gained more experience with multiple ascents, I never was completely fearless. However, I could reduce my fear of heights by visualizing being in a difficult situation on the side of the mountain (about to fall) and taking the appropriate steps to solve the problem. Positive imagery or cognitive rehearsal allows you to improve performance and can be used to desensitize your fear.

Physiologically speaking, violent physical confrontations elevate heart rate, increase blood pressure, increase sweating, tighten muscles, sharpen or redirect senses. Does this sound like something else, maybe physical exercise? Why is physical conditioning mandatory for military, law enforcement and protective agents? It better prepares them for what to expect.

In addition to the mental health benefits, physical health benefits, and social health benefits of exercise, you would also enjoy certain survivability benefits gained by regular physical exercise.

Under duress of a fearful incident, your body's primary stress hormones —adrenaline, cortisol and norepinephrine – can give you a boost of energy and focus. Physical exercise is one of the best things you can do to aid in your body's production and release of these hormones.

You can control your fear or allow your fear to control you. Fear can be effectively managed by simply changing the way you look at it.

Defining fear and looking at it from the psychological, physiological, neurological and philosophical perspectives provides an informative overview of what it is and how it works, but how exactly can you *control* it?

It's a physiological fact that fear can cause you to freeze in your tracks. How can you appropriately respond if this happens to you? Follow the example of the T1Gs and world-class competitors, take deep cleansing breaths and crack a joke.

If you choose to be more proactive in managing your fear, accept that fear is an emotion – something you own. It is a personal possession to do with as you wish. You always have a choice – allow or don't allow yourself to experience the emotion. You can detach yourself from your emotions as is often done in the DoD and LEO[77] communities.

---

77   Law Enforcement Officer(s)

Become familiarized with fear as to cause your mind to start inoculating you from the physiological effects of violent encounters. Use cognitive rehearsal (visualization) and training to help desensitize yourself from fear.

Lastly, adopt some type of physical exercise. Even if it's just a walk down the street once a day to help support your own body's health and fitness simultaneously enjoying the long-term benefits of a more well-adjusted personal security lifestyle.

Living in the new normal does not mean that you must live in fear. Paranoia is counterproductive to a healthy and sustainable level of personal security. By understanding the mechanics of fear and maintaining proper mindset, you can remain resilient in the face of danger.

EPILOGUE

YOU ARE NEVER UNARMED

> "You may not
> always carry a
> weapon,
> but you can
> always be armed."
> **STEVE TARANI**

You may not always carry a weapon, but you can always be armed. Just because you don't have a gun or practice martial arts doesn't mean you can't be both comfortable and prepared in the new normal. Now formally trained, and as part of your everyday carry, your most powerful weapon can *always* be at the ready for your personal security.

Look at all the knowledge and skills you have gained here in your training:

You know and accept the fact that you live in the *New Normal*, which increases your threat awareness and decreases your vulnerability.

You know that *Normalcy Bias* is the device retaining your most powerful weapon. You know that it can be easily defeated by knowing what it is, how it affects you, and how to use training to bypass its affect.

You know that you will not rise to the level of your expectations but fall to the level of your training. Knowledge is power. Its only practical application of that knowledge that builds skills and applying those skills builds confidence.

You know the difference between *soft targets* and *hard targets* as well as the difference between *hard skills* and *soft skills* – both of which are perishable and require maintenance. You now understand why soft skills apply to ninety percent of active threat problem solving, while hard skills apply to only the remaining ten percent.

You know that human aggression is rated on a *Scale of Injury*, and why it is a tactical imperative to sustain minimal injuries and remain combat effective.

You know that the cavalry is not going to ride over the hill to save the day and have adopted the most effective mindset in that personal security is *your* responsibility. You know that no one else will handle it for you.

You know that finding your passion (heart), building your perseverance (will) and developing your resilience (strength) provide you the mental toughness needed to unleash your most powerful weapon.

You accept the fact that bad things happen and that they could happen today, not some far-off imagined date. You have the willingness to take action against a specific person or persons if needed, and you can play the "What if" game (have a plan). Because of these, you know how to think like, act like and be a hard target.

You know that part of managing any *active threat* is about taking control of your environment by applying your situational awareness in raising or lowering your personal security radar setting based on input from your immediate surroundings. Situational awareness is not something you can afford to omit from your daily routine. As a soft skill, it must be practiced daily for it to be effective. Situational awareness doesn't cost you anything, but its benefits are immeasurable.

You understand that *threat recognition* happens when you use your five senses as well as your sixth sense plus your primal instincts to spot *threat indicators*.

You've placed another tool in your tool kit to spot anomalies and irregular behavior, by setting and looking for events occurring above or below your baseline. You can even activate your own personal security public warning system by monitoring changes in baseline rhythms.

You know the A answer to any threat is to avoid that threat altogether by stepping off those railroad tracks and not placing yourself in harm's way in the first place.

Fig. 25. Stay off the Tracks!

You now have the same tools the professionals use to support and assist them with avoiding, or mitigating a real-world threat such as using the *OODA Loop reactively* to retake the initiative and *proactively*, to prevent it from being taken.

In addition to OODA you know what is and how a *Threat Progression* and the *Attack Cycle* work together to make up the *Bad Guy's Blueprint* which affords you the opportunity to predict and even prevent an undesired event.

You know what is and where is, *bang* along a *threat progression timeline*, and why it's so critical to apply your soft skills *left of bang*[78] before being forced into using only your hard skills at the right of bang to solve the tactical problem.

---

78   Van Horne and Riley

You know that by applying proactive measures, you can increase your chances of a predator looking for a softer target. You know that by applying active measures, you can make the predator ask himself, "Are there softer targets?" and answer, "Yes!"

You know that by applying reactive measures, you can be such a burr under his fur, that the bear will drop the sharp, pointy object (you!) like a bad habit and go after softer targets.

You understand the value of *proactive measures* and *active measures* using *the 90% Advantage* over being left with only *reactive measures.*

You know that if you wait too long to avoid or mitigate a threat using your *soft skills*, that you will be forced to defend against it using your *hard skills.*

You know how to defeat an attack by affecting any one of the three anatomical elements of a successful attack. You know how to affect the target proactively by *eliminating soft target indicators.* You know what is, and how to keep INFOSEC[79]. You know how to actively affect the bad guy by *denying his opportunity* and you know how to reactively affect the attack process (step 5 of the *Attack Cycle*) by taking flight or, if there are no other options then fighting your way out.

You know what fear is, how it works, and how to control it. Using that knowledge, you know how to either *reactively* break from, or *proactively* avoid, being frozen by fear.

---

79   Information Security

Chance favors the prepared. Compare what you now know to the person standing in front of you in line at the grocery store who has *none* of the above, not one thing, not a clue as to how to handle or even identify an active threat. They are completely unprepared, and as such have compromised their own personal security. They don't realize that they have a powerful weapon on board and that it can be trained to keep them safe. This contrast demonstrates the stark difference between those who are prepared and those who don't know, don't care, don't want to know (unprepared) or are living in denial.

Knowing what you know, builds your mental toughness, makes you a hard target, and decreases your vulnerability. You may not have a gun or be versed in the martial arts, but you are now well equipped to live comfortably and handle bad things that happen to good people in the new normal. Using your most powerful weapon, from here on out, you are *never* unarmed.

CONTINUING EDUCATION

How can you continue your training?

You can attend professional instructor-led training – SteveTarani.com

Keep informed – sign up for your free Open Source Intelligence (OSINT) newsletter delivered via email at no cost – SteveTarani.com

Learn more about Preventative Defense - book a class with either myself or a certified PreFense Instructor in your area. PreventativeDefense.com

If you may have any further questions you can always reach me at:

Steve@ SteveTarani.com

Hope to see you in future training!

Stay safe,

Steve

GLOSSARY

Action-Reaction Power Curve - Reaction always follows action, and this is the reason why you need to reduce your reaction time as much as possible.

Active Measures - Causing activity or change characterized by action rather than by contemplation.

Active Shooter - An armed person who has used deadly physical force on other persons and continues to do so while having unrestricted access to additional victims.

Active Threat – A term attributed to anything bad that can happen to you anywhere or anytime that can potentially cause physical or financial injury or death.

Actor - A participant in an attack.

Anatomy of an Attack - The component parts of a successful attack and how they work together minimally requiring three items: 1. A bad guy 2. A target 3. A means or process of executing that attack. Eliminate one item and you dissolve the attack.

Attack Behavior - The observable activity of stalking, closing in on, and attacking a target.

Attack Cycle - A universal five-step process comprised of defined steps which must be followed by any predator to complete a successful attack.

Avoidance - Is nothing more than stepping off those railroad tracks and not putting yourself in front of that freight train (active threat) in the first place. It is a proactive measure.

Bad Guy's Blueprint - How an event will occur. Knowing the Bad Guy's Blueprint allows you to predict what is coming next and how to handle it.

Bang - "If you were to think of an attack on a timeline, bang is in the middle. Bang is the act. Bang is the IED [Improvised Explosive Device] explosion, the sniper taking the shot, or the beginning of an ambush. Bang is what we want to prevent. Being left of bang means that a person has observed the pre-event indicators, one of the warning signs, that must occur earlier on the timeline for the bang to happen."[80]

Baseline - Items and/or people in your environment that you consider normal or normal behavior. (Example: The baseline of a coffee shop would be baristas making coffee, patrons sitting at tables reading or on their laptops, people in line ordering their drinks, etc.)

Color Code - The first component of using your Situational Awareness to control your environment. Developed by Colonel Cooper in the 1960s, there are four colors representing varied conditions of awareness applied to environmental observation which were adopted by the US Defense, Intelligence and law enforcement communities. You can think of these as settings on your personal security radar, where you can click up or down to any one of the four.

---

80 Left of Bang – How the Marine Corps' Combat Hunter Program Can Save Your Life" Page 15-16

Condition Orange - If you happen to observe a potential threat, you are placed on mental alert and click up a notch on your personal security radar. It is the third level of the Color Code. In this condition, you have identified a specific threat.

Condition Red - This is the highest setting on your radar of the Color Code. It means that you are now in the fight. As things have now gone physical (to the right of bang), you are called to physical action. A condition where you have no other option but to use your hard skills.

Condition White - The lowest setting of the Color Code representing the lowest level of awareness. This setting describes when you are comfortably at home with doors locked, perfectly safe and in a completely controlled environment replete with locks, alarms, cameras, firewalls, etc.

Condition Yellow - This is the second level on the Color Code. Representing a condition of awareness where you are prepared and aware of your surroundings. It is a recommended default setting when you are in public.

Contact Range - Moving so close to your opponent that they can make physical contact with you. It is a personal distance where injury begins.

De-escalate, Deter, Defuse - Protective measures utilized to help break the attack cycle at the later steps.

Defense - This is when you can no longer avoid or mitigate the threat. It begins when your soft skills are no longer applicable. It is a reactive measure.

Edged Weapons - Includes the likes of steak or kitchen knives, razor blades, broken glass, improvised weapons fashioned from common objects such as coat hangers or soup cans, used in such a manner as to de-escalate, defuse, and otherwise deter a physical attack.

Event Indicator - An observable pre-event activity preceding every action. Examples of this include someone taking a breath before they speak or moving a foot over the brake pedal before braking.

Fight - One of three defensive options when engaging a physical threat, counterattack; do whatever it takes using anything at your disposal to put yourself in a condition where you can eventually move off the X. In terms of the Scale of Human Aggression, a fight is also the iconic barroom brawl, two kids fighting after school or a fight between players during a game represent typical examples of this mid-level physical expression of human aggression. A fight can result in significant physical injury.

Flexible Weapon - Includes the likes of purse straps, computer cables, your t-shirt, lengths of rope, etc.

Flight - When engaging a physical threat, move off the X. Increase the Reactionary Gap by placing distance and/or objects between yourself and the threat.

Flight, Fight or Freeze - A protective concept describing the three immediate reactions we, as humans, may have in response to a life-threatening challenge.

Gray Man - A term attributed to the Defense Intelligence community describing persons trained in the art of blending into the environment as part of the performance of their job.

Hard Skills - Your physical capabilities that directly apply to your physically surviving personal combat (i.e. hand-to-hand combat, firearms proficiency, defensive driving).

Hard Targets - Those who are aware of their environment know that bad things happen, and such threats can be addressed with threat management and protection.

Heart - Also known as passion. It is an intense and over-powering feeling or conviction that provides the driving force behind your intentions.

Improvised Weapons - Anything you can hold in your hands under duress and in threatening circumstances that could be used to defend yourself against a physical assault. Also known as weapons of opportunity.

Information Security (INFOSEC) – Controlling information out, whether it be audio or visual information.

Lone Wolf Attack - An attack conducted without leadership. The lone wolf predominantly operates per his namesake without any direct supervision. Usually with no other actors and, often with minimal or no funding, the lone wolf is forced to do everything himself.

Mental Toughness - An inner strength that resides somewhere in the depth of your being, affording you the confidence to overcome anxiety. Mental toughness is a measure of individual resilience and confidence that can predict success in the workplace, sport, competition and under extreme pressure. It refers to any set of positive attributes that helps you to cope with and perform under duress and in difficult situations.

Mitigation - This is what you do to limit the cascading of negative effects of an undesired event already in motion. It is an active measure.

Move off the X - Using this reactive measure as an immediate response option, you may quickly remove yourself from harm's way and get to safety.

Non-Contact Range - Being out of physical reach of your opponent.

Normalcy Bias - This is a mental state you enter when confronted with an overwhelming threat. It makes you disbelieve your situation when faced with grave and imminent danger.[81] This phenomenon causes you to greatly underestimate the severity and the most likely consequences. This, in turn, causes you to reinterpret the event instead of taking evasive or decisive action.

OODA Loop - An acronym derived from a combination of four dynamic decision-making steps: Observe, Orient, Decide, and Act. A reactive measure designed to help you stay ahead of the action-reaction power curve and make rapid, compressed, definitive and appropriate decisions more quickly than your adversary.

Personal Combat - This is the very highest level on the scale of human aggression. Here, you are literally fighting for your life. Usually involving weapons such as guns or knives, they are trying to kill you and it is either you or him/them.

---

81   International Journal of Mass Emergencies and Disaster, Nov. 1988, Vol 6, No. 3, PP 315

Personal Weapons - Includes your closed fists, open palms, and knees. They are used in such a manner as to de-escalate, defuse and otherwise deter a physical attack.

Potential Threat - An environment, situation, area, activity, or person(s) perceived as possibly dangerous or harmful.

Pre-Attack Behaviors - Activities a predator engages in to prepare for an attack, such as searching for, choosing, and beginning to stalk a target.

Predator's Optic - Predators see the world as made up of either soft targets or hard targets. Whenever possible, a predator will shy away from hard targets and focus his/her attention on less protected targets.

Preventative Measures - Actions or activities resulting in avoidance or mitigation of an active threat.

Proactive Measures - Protective measures which are utilized in threat management and protection to avoid, mitigate, or defend against a threat before it turns into an attack.

Protectee - A person who is being protected.

Protective Agent - A trained professional whose job it is to provide personal security for an assigned person or persons.

Protective Intelligence - The art and science of collecting and assessing relevant information about adversaries who may have the interest, motive, intention, opportunity and capability of mounting attacks against you and the things you care about.

Reactionary Gap - A protective concept defining the relationship between distance and time. The shorter distance between you and the threat, the less time you have to respond. Conversely, the greater the distance, the greater the amount of time.

Reactive Measures - Those protective measures which may be employed in response to an attack.

Resource Assessment Listing - A mental checklist of those items in your immediate environment, and within arm's reach, that can be utilized to stop another person presenting a physical threat.

Scale of Human Aggression - Physical human aggression that is measured on a scale from lowest to highest intensity.

Scale of Injury - There are five levels of physical injury with the lowest being no injury at all, which is the very best possible outcome of engaging a physical threat.

Scuffle - Mildest physical expression. Triggered by verbal insults, challenges, or similar combination of confrontational communication, a scuffle sits at the bottom of the Scale of Human Aggression. You may likely observe this physical expression in the form of finger-pointing, grabbing of collars, shoving or pushing.

Situational Awareness - Maintaining a relaxed condition of observance for any threat indicators and being prepared to appropriately respond. Being aware of your surroundings.

Soft Skills - These are concepts. Soft skills are gained by awareness-based training, to include applying your situational awareness and your ability to recognize a threat.

Soft Targets - Those who are unaware, disregard, or do not care that bad things happen and/or are unaware of their environment and/or unaware of threat management and protection and/or unprepared to protect themselves.

Soft Target Indicators - Any appearance or activity outwardly exhibited indicator that screams, "Hey look over here. I'm an easy target. Pick me!" to a predator. These can also be further classified into primary (awareness based) and secondary (preparedness based) soft target indicators.

Strength - Also known as resiliency. Resiliency is the mental capacity to recover quickly from difficulties. It is the temper of mental toughness. Bouncing back when things get ugly gives you confidence which makes you stronger.

Threat Avoidance - Very simply put; don't be there in the first place. Do not intentionally place yourself in harm's way.

Threat Indicators - Anything you observe about your environment that triggers a concern that conditions have changed from non-threatening to threatening and indicates a need for your attention.

Threat Progression - A step process ranging from a potential threat to an active threat to pre-attack behaviors to attack behaviors that demonstrates the transition of threat through recognizable stages. A predictable timeline of foreseeable events.

Threat Recognition - How to recognize a threat.

Will - Also known as perseverance. The Merriam-Webster dictionary definition of perseverance is "continued effort to do or achieve something despite difficulties, failure, or opposition." Perseverance is the hammer that forges mental toughness.